W9-CSY-737

BLESSED,
DONALD J. TRUMP,
AND THE
SPIRITUAL WAR

BLESSED, DONALD J. TRUMP, ### AND THE # SPIRITUAL WAR

HOW THE BATTLE FOR THE SOUL OF
THIS COUNTRY BEGAN WITH ONE WORD

BOB UNANUE

Post Hill
PRESS

A POST HILL PRESS BOOK
ISBN: 979-8-88845-836-5
ISBN (eBook): 979-8-88845-837-2

Blessed, Donald J. Trump, and the Spiritual War:
How the Battle for the Soul of This Country Began with One Word
© 2024 by Bob Unanue
All Rights Reserved

Cover design by Priscilla Allyson Brito

Post Hill Press
New York • Nashville
posthillpress.com

Published in the United States of America
1 2 3 4 5 6 7 8 9 10

For Dad,
who raised us in the faith and left us this Gospel verse
before he passed in March of 1976. John 13:33–34:
"My children, I will be with you only a little longer.
You will look for me…where I am going, you cannot
come. A new command I give you: love one another
as I have loved you, so you must love one another."

For Mom,

who, through her unconditional love and dedication
to her husband and children, provided a home of
privilege; not of money or material things, rather,
a home where we truly felt loved and valued.

For my children and grandchildren,
La Gran Familia Goya,
and everyone who recognizes the value of family.

TABLE OF CONTENTS

FOREWORD

One of the first times I met Bob Unanue was at the White House in July of 2020—a turbulent time, for those who remember. This was in the midst of the COVID-19 pandemic and the George Floyd riots, and we were leading up to one of the most important elections in our nation's history.

In the midst of this uncertainty, President Donald Trump called Bob up to the Rose Garden podium on that sunny summer day, the president and CEO of Goya Foods, and the author of this book.

It is not hyperbole to say that Bob's remarks that day captivated not just the audience in front of him, but the nation as a whole. Bob spoke from the heart and shared a powerful message of gratitude for the blessings of life and liberty in America, and his hopes for the future of our country in which those same values could flourish.

Predictably, he was attacked for embracing conservative values and President Trump's accomplishments that day. As I have come to know all too well, the Democrat Party becomes absolutely incensed when minorities think for themselves, because it goes against their entire political agenda. The Left wants to keep us divided—by race, by class, by sex, by religion, and everything else you can think of. Bob's message was exactly the opposite of that: we are one nation, one peo-

11

ple, united as children under one glorious Creator—and we should come together to embrace each other and stand up for our values rather than let the voices of division convince us that we are each other's enemies.

When a Hispanic American or African American sheds those arbitrary groups and instead calls on us to embrace our shared values as American citizens, the Left attacks because it threatens the very source of their power and control. The attacks are outlandish, unfair, radical, and often even racially charged—but of course, the media gives them a pass, and the cycle continues. Welcome to the world of national politics, Bob!

After that day, I decided that Bob was someone I would have to get to know better. I soon came to realize that Bob was the perfect embodiment of the American Dream. He grew up in suburban New Jersey, where his family spoke English, despite the fact that his father was a second-generation immigrant. In the Unanue household, they spoke English because they wanted to embrace American values and American culture.

Bob took over Goya Foods in 2004, making him the third-generation Unanue to run the company. Under Bob, Goya Foods achieved stunning growth, and is now the largest Hispanic-owned food producer in the country.

Bob loves our country, he loves our values, and above all, he loves our Creator. He gives back to those around him, he invests in our future, and he uses his blessings to do everything in his power to build a better future for our children and grandchildren. Through faith, hard work, and determination, Bob has built not only a wonderful life for himself, but he has also lifted up all those around him along the way. He never relied on government to get where he is today, and he knows firsthand the power of the free market and the ingenuity that is unleashed when government steps back out of the way.

The media attacked Bob after those remarks not because he did anything wrong; it was because he did everything right. Most of all, they attacked Bob because he had the courage to stand up for what he believes—and for inspiring others to do the same. Of course, their attacks backlashed; the Goya Foods "boycott" quickly turned into a "buy-cott," and sales boomed after Bob's Rose Garden appearance. The silent majority stepped up to the plate once again.

I am honored to call Bob a fellow patriot in the fight to save our country, a cornerstone trustee of my organization, the American Cornerstone Institute, and above all, a friend.

This book is a magnificent achievement, albeit one of many great accomplishments throughout his life. It tells a story of perseverance, hard work, courage, faith, and God's guiding hand.

Bob's story gives us wisdom to draw from as we navigate the turbulent days ahead, and his life's example offers us inspiration for our own lives.

I hope you enjoy this book, learn from its examples, and take its lessons to heart. God bless you, and God bless our great nation.

—*Dr. Ben Carson*

INTRODUCTION

The road to truth, God, and ultimately, salvation is never an easy one to follow. It is fraught with challenges, criticism, disbelief, and contempt. Saint Matthew put it best, "For wide is the gate and broad is the road that leads to destruction, and many enter through it. But small is the gate and narrow the road that leads to life, and only a few find it." I've spent my life trying to walk that narrow road by rooting every decision I've ever made in the principles of God, family, and work—the very same principles that guided my father Anthony, who diligently passed them on to each of his children. As a devout Catholic, my belief in God and the Holy Spirit has never wavered despite the incredible pushback, criticism, disbelief, and contempt I have received along the way.

You likely know me because of my company, Goya Foods, the largest privately owned Hispanic food company in America. Or maybe you know me from what has become a seminal moment in my life—a Rose Garden event at the White House on July 9, 2020, which changed my life forever.

On that day, I had been invited to speak alongside President Donald Trump at the announcement of the White House Hispanic Prosperity Initiative, which—after years of work by me, Syddia Lee-Chee, my longtime external affairs consultant in Washington, DC, and other prominent Hispanic leaders—

was created by the Trump administration to give Hispanic Americans greater access to educational and economic opportunities. When I stepped into the Rose Garden, I was resolute on one thing—our country, my country, had taken a turn for the worse, not just for Hispanics but for all Americans. The COVID-19 pandemic had all but killed the hardworking American spirit upon which this country was founded. Although Goya remained open as an essential business, thousands of companies closed, creating a shutdown of our economy, which would cripple the work ethic and prosperity of our great country.

For the record, I submit that *all* businesses are essential.

People were hurting—some couldn't put food on the table. So, in addition to the announcement of the White House Hispanic Prosperity Initiative, I would also be announcing that Goya was donating two million pounds of food for our country. (In actuality, it ended up doubling to more than four million pounds.) As a person of faith who loves America, this represented a true honor and privilege.

The Rose Garden was especially gorgeous on that warm summer afternoon. There I was under a cloudless blue sky standing next to the leader of the free world. It was an incredible feeling. In the shadow of the grand columns, surrounded by white and pink rose shrubs, in the same spot where so many dignitaries had stood over the years, I spoke of my grandfather, Prudencio Unanue, who founded Goya and laid the groundwork for the company that we know and love today. He was a true visionary who lived his life as a builder—a man who created from nothing what we call "this great family" or "La Gran Familia," basically the thousands of people who make up Goya.

What happened next, well, it was nothing short of a miracle.

With President Trump standing to my left and the gaggle of cameras and news reporters assigned to the White House beat before me, I was overcome by the Holy Spirit. The president introduced me and as I began speaking, the words that came from my lips weren't necessarily my own—they came from divine intervention. I opened my mouth and out came, "We are all truly *blessed* to have a leader like President Trump, who is a builder, and that's what my grandfather did. He came to this country to build, to grow, to prosper. And so, we have an incredible builder, and we pray. We pray for our leadership, our president, and we pray for our country, that we will continue to prosper and to grow."

"Blessed."

The Holy Spirit compelled me to use that word. And I obeyed. But the backlash for doing so came quickly. People who were shocked, dismayed, offended (or all three) that I used the words "blessed" and "President Trump" in the same sentence called for a boycott of Goya products, with the loudest voice coming from a sitting United States congresswoman—a Latina, by the way. The hashtags #BoycottGoya and #Goyaway began trending on social media. News outlets reported on the public outcry and the relentless calls for me to apologize. I'd get calls from these organizations, acting as though they were some sort of tribunal, to come before them and kneel and apologize. I wasn't about to do that.

I was sentenced by cancel culture. It came with insults, threats, and a barrage of four-letter words aimed not just at me but also my children and grandchildren. But as the Apostle Paul wrote in 2 Corinthians, "Persecuted but not abandoned, cast down but not destroyed." God-fearing people, the same ones who put President Trump in the Oval Office in the first place, began buying Goya products in droves. Our sales exploded. What began as a boycott morphed into a "buycott." Marketing experts estimate the media coverage gave Goya nearly $200 million in "earned media" or basically, free advertising. This not only supported Goya as a company but also sent a loud and profound message that God does have a voice. It demonstrated His unmitigated power. There is no human way the reaction could have been so enormous without the hand of God, the Holy Spirit.

The hail of negativity surrounding the words that God brought to my lips can only be described as the incarnation of evil. It's just so telling that on a day when President Trump announced an initiative to help Hispanics, nefarious people tried to destroy a family-owned Hispanic business. That's evil. We were attacked by invoking God, and I didn't have any control over what would happen to me or Goya. But God protected us. Good always overcomes evil.

Nothing I said was untrue. We, as a nation, *are* truly blessed. Everything that has happened to me was God sent. The voice of the Holy Spirit *cannot* be silenced.

The series of events that transpired next would change the course and purpose of my life. I was thrust into a limelight brighter than any I had ever encountered. I have since appeared on major television news programs across the country, been written about in a myriad of newspapers and websites. I have faced countless questions about my choice of words on that fateful, sunny day in the Rose Garden. I have been asked about why I refused to apologize to the cancel mob that wanted to destroy me and my company. Easy answer—you never, ever apologize for obeying God and doing the things He's called you to do and speak. As an aside, for any business leader who stands upon principle, never, ever give in to the cancel mob; all that does is empower it. Have the courage to stand on your beliefs, stand on your principles, and know that in the end your integrity won't be the only thing intact, your business likely will be too. I'm proof.

God has led me places where I might never have ventured otherwise. He put a hunger for helping children upon my heart. I was drawn to the plight of those children who suffer at the hands of evil, being trafficked around the world—a multibillion dollar business with the biggest consumers here in our own backyard. Thinking of my own six children and fourteen grandchildren who are the light of my life, I was propelled by the Holy Spirit to bring awareness to this truth—that the children of God cannot be sold. We began an initiative called Goya Cares to reach out to the victims of child trafficking and children who are suffering from mental illness so that they may have hope to live in a world where their life is valued. We try to safeguard children by raising awareness through education and prevention efforts. God opened the door for me to be an executive producer of a wildly successful motion picture that alerted the masses to the dangers of child trafficking—the blockbuster 2023 film, *Sound of Freedom*. And as the character Vampiro, played by the incredibly talented Bill Camp, says in the film, "When God tells you what to do, you cannot hesitate." So I did not hesitate to answer the call.

It's been an extraordinary ride since that July day in 2020. Opportunities I never could have created for myself have come in abundance and I have seized them. It's much like what Morgan Freeman, as God, articulates in the 2007 film, *Evan Almighty*. He says, "Let me ask you something. If someone prays for patience, you think God gives them patience? Or does he give them the opportunity to be patient? If he prayed for courage, does God give him courage, or does he give him opportunities to be courageous? If someone prayed for the family to be closer, do you think God zaps them with warm fuzzy feelings, or does he give them opportunities to love each other?" And that's what happened to me. God gave me the opportunity to stand for Him and I took it. Now, one day I'm given an opportunity to help produce a motion picture, and the next I'm on television talking about the state of the country and our need to return to God. How does this happen? The Holy Spirit. And why me? I don't know. I'm not an overly religious "Holy Roller," but I do know this: He has a message—America must get back to the godly principals upon which it was founded—and if I can be a vessel to spread that message, here am I. Send me.

This book will detail every act of the Holy Spirit that has been channeled through me, and how He continues to use me as a vessel to trumpet the clarion call that America must return to the principles that made it the greatest nation in the whole of humankind.

And it all began with one word—

"Blessed."

In the Beginning

CHAPTER 1

OUR PLANS AREN'T ALWAYS GOD'S PLANS.

"Der Mensch Tracht, Un Gott Lacht."
Translation: "Man plans, and God laughs."
—*Yiddish proverb*

Man plans and God laughs. Yes, that old Yiddish expression is true. So many of us plan our lives according to *our* purpose that we're often blinded to the reality that our plans aren't necessarily God's plans. But when we least expect it, and in ways we never see coming, God tells us it's time to execute *His* plan for us. That's exactly what happened to me. Despite my carefully honed blueprint of working unobtrusively as the CEO of Goya, God had another plan—to take me from my behind-the-scenes comfort zone to a huge, public platform from which to spread His message. When He says it's time to move, you move.

I never imagined any of it. I never thought I'd be a somewhat regular staple on cable news. Who could have seen that coming? Not me. I run a food company. Could I have imagined phone calls with the president of the United States? No, I couldn't. But here's the special sauce—

God could.

Man plans and God laughs, indeed.

God has opened doors I never could have opened myself. I wouldn't have that ability. I'd never be able to get tens of thousands of rosaries with a message of love, faith, and hope into war-torn Ukraine on my own. But I've done just that. I never envisioned being on a White House commission or as an executive producer of a Hollywood blockbuster. I've now done both. That's how God works sometimes—seemingly insurmountable undertakings assigned to us for which He provides completely. You must be led by faith and belief—not just in Him, but in the knowledge that whatever His task, it'll be bigger and more profound than anything you could have imagined on your own. You can never outdream God.

No opportunity since that afternoon in the Rose Garden came about just because I'm Bob Unanue. No, as the Apostle Paul wrote to the Philippians, "For it is God who works in you to will and to act in order to fulfill his good purpose." God plucked me from obscurity and gave me a platform—a massive platform. But He often uses what you already have to help fulfill His plans for you. Had I not been the CEO of Goya, I likely wouldn't have had the credibility to approach the president of the United States about anything.

As the CEO of Goya, I hoped to push the Trump administration to be more involved in the empowerment of Hispanic communities nationwide. It's the goal I've had with every presidential administration. The United States is the second largest Latino country in the world after Mexico, but sadly no administration had gotten that close to our community.

Then God opened the door.

Trump appointed me as a member of the President's Advisory Commission on Hispanic Prosperity. What an incredible honor. The night before we'd be announcing the Hispanic Prosperity Initiative in the Rose Garden (the day I said "blessed") I'd flown into Washington and checked into the Trump International Hotel on Pennsylvania Avenue, which was just a stone's throw away from the White House. The hotel has since been sold and rebranded as a Waldorf Astoria. But on that day, the grandeur of what was once the iconic Old Post Office amplified my nervous excitement over a scheduled roundtable in the Cabinet Room that included, among others, President Trump, Jeanette Nuñez, the lieutenant governor of Florida, Jovita Carranza, the forty-fourth treasurer of the United States and the head of the Small Business Administration, Betsy DeVos, the secretary of education, Dan Garza of the LIBRE Initiative, former New Mexico lieutenant governor John Sanchez, and Mexican actor, filmmaker, and political activist, Eduardo Verástegui.

I'd been to the White House before, but whether it's one time or a hundred, for any true and patriotic American, entering the gates at 1600 Pennsylvania Avenue is a thrill not accurately described in words, and knowing you're about to meet with some of the most powerful people in the world to engage in helping the Hispanic community, well, that's another level of awe...and gratitude.

When I walked into the Cabinet Room, I saw the huge conference table, around which many of history's most important conversations had taken place. There was the draping, the flags, and the gathered dignitaries. I was excited, nervous, and proud, all at the same time. As I looked around the room, trying to digest it all, I could only imagine what my late father would have thought if he'd have known his son would one day be sitting in the Cabinet Room next to the president of the United States.

I didn't have much time to ponder any of that before President Trump entered the room. He's as charismatic a man as you're ever likely to meet and his presence certainly filled the entire space. All of us who were seated around the large table were sort of caught up in the enormity of the moment, and before I could say anything, the president, who had yet to take his seat, turned in my direction and said, "That's the best-looking guy on the planet—better looking than Clark Gable!" We all just started laughing. Okay, full disclosure— Eduardo was seated next to me, and if you've ever seen him, you'd agree, he is a very good-looking man.

Anyway, the president settled in, and as good fortune would have it, I'd been assigned a seat next to him, on his right side. As the conversation moved around the room, with each of us seated at the table sharing a quick comment or two, I was thinking about what I would say. I had nothing scripted and figured I'd just speak off the cuff. That approach has served me pretty well over the years. Though I didn't know exactly what I would say, the one thing I did know was that God's hand was on me. I mean, all of a sudden I go from obscurity to being a part of a presidential commission to now being seated at the right hand of the president of the United States—the best spot in the room. That is, without doubt, the hand of God.

After everyone else had spoken, it was now my turn to speak. It would be an understatement to say I was nervous. Besides the gathered dignitaries and the president, there was the White House press corps, all wearing medical masks since this was in the midst of the pandemic, and a bank of television cameras now trained on me too. I began with some pleasantries, my expression of gratitude for being there, and the thrill that Goya as a whole had for this new initiative. In the news footage from that day, one might not know it to look at me, but I was busting at the seams with excitement over the progress we'd made in helping Hispanic empowerment. One minute and nineteen seconds after I finished speaking, the roundtable adjourned, and the gaggle of reporters began screaming questions at the president as the press office began moving them down to the Rose Garden where my life would change after I spoke one particular word.

What most people don't know, given the partisan hoopla surrounding my using the word "blessed," is that Trump isn't the first sitting president I'd worked with. Back in 2012, I was honored to have Goya join First Lady Michelle Obama's "Let's Move" initiative to promote MiPlato, the Spanish translation of "MyPlate," to help promote healthy eating and to help alleviate hunger in the Hispanic community.

"Everything that Goya is doing, from the MiPlato posters and pamphlets to cookbooks and recipes, center around the idea that we parents can make simple changes to help their children lead healthier lives," said Mrs. Obama, when our partnership was first announced. We worked for years with the Obama administration with great success. It didn't matter to me that he was a Democrat. Conversely, it didn't matter to me whether Trump was a Republican. When the president calls, you answer. Period. Political party never mattered to me. These days, respect for the office has gone by the wayside—swept out to sea by waves of division and hate.

I'd once proudly introduced Barack Obama at a White House event in 2011 and told the gathered crowd how I was "honored and humbled and deeply grateful" to be there with him. I further added, "It's my great honor and privilege to present to you the president of the United States, who, by being the first African American president, represents the diversity that makes this country so unique and the greatest nation in the world. Ladies and gentleman, President Barack Obama." Watching the mainstream media in the wake of my Rose Garden comments, would anybody have known that I did that? Of course not, it wasn't news. No one called for a boycott of Goya. Conservatives weren't screaming bloody murder and trying to get me fired. In fact, no one from any political persuasion tried to cancel me or demand I apologize. There was no earned media. Not a dime. No doors opened. I wasn't propelled into ubiquity nor given a platform. Here's why (besides the media's long-standing anti-conservative bias and the fact that conservatives don't cancel people for diversity of thought). There's a phrase in the book of Esther that says, "...for such a time as this." What it basically means is that God has His perfect time, His perfect moment, where He calls us to our true purpose—to make a profound difference. So the Rose Garden event with Trump was the "such a time as this."

Funny how God always seems to pick what we'd consider the most *imperfect* time to call us into His purpose. But His timing is always *perfect*.

My original plan for meeting Trump was to host him at our Goya distribution center just outside of Houston, Texas, a couple of months prior to my ending up at the White House. I planned to announce a huge food donation to the country and wanted the president there. During this time, we'd been working with food banks, food pantries, soup kitchens, and other partner organizations to make sure the food was distributed directly to the people facing food insecurity and hardships from the direct impact of the pandemic. And due to the pandemic, the president's team called off the visit. The giant American flag we proudly hung for the occasion still hangs in the distribution center.

God's timing is always *perfect*.

The Rose Garden comments. "Blessed." Trump. All of them were the result of God's perfect timing. The Holy Spirit triggered interviews; triggered talking about God on a very public stage; triggered being offered a rosary that turned into thousands of rosaries; triggered being sent to Poland, on the border of Ukraine, and sending those rosaries into Ukraine; triggered creating Goya Cares and raising awareness of child trafficking; triggered *Sound of Freedom* and my involvement in it; triggered my new lifelong calling.

And the Holy Spirit will trigger a spiritual renaissance in America.

CHAPTER 2

CANCELED? NEVER.

*"To see him attacked, the Goya president, by those
who would censor him, those who would 'woke'
him, is very disappointing but entirely predictable."*

—*Geraldo Rivera on Fox News*

M y story, at least this chapter in my life, is a powerful, inspirational story of divine protection, faith, and courage. But in the moments during the Rose Garden speech, I didn't know any of that nor what evil would be awaiting me.

Once we'd wrapped up things at the White House, I returned to the hotel. What a day! I was basking in the glow of a day gone very, very well—I mean, come on, the president had just signed a huge initiative and I'd been appointed to a commission that would help Hispanics to prosper. Yes. It had been a great day.

Then the phone rang.

A producer from Fox News was on the line asking me to appear on the next morning's *Fox & Friends* to discuss the controversy. Controversy? What controversy? I honestly had no idea what they were talking about. But as if on cue, rapid-fire text message alerts began lighting up my phone. Goya had become a victim of cancel culture run amuck.

Prominent Hispanic voices were calling for a boycott of our products. Julian Castro, the former secretary of Housing and Urban Development under Obama tweeted, "Goya Foods has been a staple of so many Latino households for generations. Now their CEO, Bob Unanue, is praising a president who villainizes and maliciously attacks Latinos for political gain. Americans should think twice before buying their products." Representative Alexandria Ocasio-Cortez weighed in too. "Oh look, it's the sound of me Googling 'how to make your own Adobo.'" And Lin-Manuel Miranda, director and star of the Broadway hit *Hamilton*, jumped on the bandwagon, writing, "We learned to bake bread in this pandemic, we can learn to make our own adobo con pimienta. Bye."

What really struck me was the venom directed at a truly Hispanic company by Hispanic people—people who likely grew up eating our products. Goya is a true Hispanic success story. What it really boiled down to was this—the president and CEO of a Hispanic company spoke positively about President Trump. They felt it was a betrayal to the community. But really, when the rubber met the road, the only people who truly felt betrayed were elites like them.

I accepted the offer to appear on *Fox & Friends*, and by the time morning rolled around, truth be told, I was strongly determined to make my point. "So, you're allowed to talk good about or to praise one president, but you're not allowed—when I was called to be part of this commission to aid in economic and educational prosperity and you make a positive comment, all of a sudden that's not acceptable," I told the panel. I made it clear I felt no remorse for being complimentary of Trump nor for accepting the invite in the first place. "If you're called by the president of the United States, you're going to say, 'No, I'm sorry, I'm busy. No thank you?' I didn't say that to the Obamas, and I didn't say that to President Trump."

A short time later during the same program Geraldo Rivera recounted how, when he was a boy, Goya products were present at almost every meal in his home, and how unfortunate it was that I was a victim of cancel culture. "To see him attacked, the Goya president, by those who would censor him, those who would 'woke' him is very disappointing but entirely predictable given the climate of the times where if you don't tow the liberal line, you get attacked six weeks to Sunday."

I found myself on CNN, ABC, CBS, MSNBC, Fox News, and essentially every major news outlet in the English-speaking world. Oh, and in the Spanish-speaking world too since I was a fixture on both Univision and Telemundo. There wasn't a single day that I wasn't on television somewhere. I woke up every day to a new headline. And social media? Forget it. I was everywhere.

The next day I agreed to be a guest on *The Ingraham Angle* on Fox News. Yes, another Fox News program. I'd been besieged with requests for comment by essentially every news network and publication, and after much thought, I'd concluded it was best to stay in the zone of "friendly fire," so to speak.

Just before introducing me, host Laura Ingraham lambasted Hispanic liberals like Alexandria Ocasio-Cortez, not just for their intolerance, but for their lack of gratitude. "Not only is AOC attempting to destroy a Hispanic success story—

she is spitting in the face of someone who has likely helped her and her constituents get fed. In the past few months alone, Goya has donated millions of pounds of food to the U.S. food banks, including 100,000 pounds to the New York City Food Bank to be distributed to families in need during the COVID-19 pandemic," Ingraham said.

She continued, comparing me to sports figures and all manner of celebrities who'd been forced to apologize for standing with President Trump, and asked whether I, too, would apologize. I boldly and proudly proclaimed, "Hell no. Hell no!"

Why would I apologize? If you apologize to these people, it only feeds and empowers them. Besides, I owed them nothing. Not a thing. It's people like AOC, Julian Castro, Lin-Manuel Miranda, and their so-called progressive ilk whose intolerance and divisiveness are destroying this country.

People like that are deranged. Truly. To destroy others over a difference of political opinion, that's twisted, and just plain evil. They were openly calling for the destruction of a business without any concern—none, whatsoever—of how it would affect the more than four thousand people employed by Goya, most of them Hispanic.

I was being threatened. My children were being threatened. My grandchildren were being threatened. Goya hired a crisis management team to mitigate damage to the brand. But as they say, a funny thing happened on the way to the forum. We never lost our core customers, and, in fact, we gained millions more.

The leftist boycott landed with a thud. I watched as Goya sales went through the roof. Literally, every day when I'd see the numbers, I'd say "Wow!" There was even a guy in Arlington, Virginia—Casey Harper, a producer for commentator Eric Bolling's show, *America This Week*—who started a GoFundMe campaign to raise money to buy our products, which he would then donate to several food pantries in the Washington, DC, area. He raised more than $300,000! Then there were the messages I'd received from so many people pledging to support Goya by buying our products. I had to laugh when one guy said to me, "I have absolutely no idea what to do with any of your products, but I'm going to the store and buying everything they've got."

One morning I got a phone call from the White House, and on the other end of the line was a chuckling President Trump who joked, "I hear I'm making you rich! Your products are flying off the shelf!" We had a good laugh. But, on a serious note, he also told me that I had courage in standing up to the bullies of cancel culture. If there's anyone who knows a thing or two about standing up to the evil forces trying to destroy you, it's most assuredly Donald Trump. The president posted a photo on Twitter (now X) of himself in the Oval Office giving a "thumbs up" to the Goya products lined up on the Resolute desk, and later a tweet with the caption, "I [heart] Goya." Even his daughter, Ivanka, showed her support for us by tweeting a photo with her holding a can of our black beans, with this incredible (and true) caption—"If it's Goya, it has to be good."

Predictably, this seemingly innocent act was criticized by left-wing nuts who, to this day, still try to claim that the president's support for Goya was illegal. I fully believe that if the Biden administration and the leftist power elites weren't so busy harassing Donald Trump with frivolous legal cases, they'd have charged him and Ivanka with corruption by now, all for daring to hold a can of Goya beans.

The extreme Left's hypocrisy is always so obvious. So, it's okay for elected officials, such as AOC, to boycott a company but not okay for elected officials to *defend* the same company?

Regardless, our sales climbed so dramatically that I decided to reward AOC, since she was one of the people responsible. That's when I named her Goya's "Employee of the Month." AOC's scheme to ruin us ended up working about as well as one of Wile E. Coyote's ACME missiles in those old Road Runner cartoons. The late radio legend, Rush Limbaugh, caught wind of what I'd done in naming AOC the "Employee of the Month" and called it out during one of his shows later that year. "I love people that think that way. I love people that react that way. It's just fabulous," he told his legions of listeners. Rush even included the story in his final book.

People like AOC are so blinded by rage that the good someone does never rises above their politics. My longtime working relationship with the Obamas meant nothing. Goya giving away millions of pounds of food to the disadvantaged meant nothing. Using the word "blessed" in the Rose Garden next to Donald Trump canceled out all that goodwill, so, in their minds, I had to be canceled. I'm sorry, but that's insane.

But here's the lesson of which they have no grasp—what God has blessed cannot be cursed. It was no accident that Goya sales blew up. How does a company go from the merciless attacks of people hellbent on destroying it to not just surviving, but *thriving*? The answer is easy—the intervention of God and the Holy Spirit.

In the Bible, the book of Daniel tells the story of three guys named Shadrach, Meshach, and Abednego. They were wise, righteous men in Babylon who, despite threats to their lives, refused to bow down to golden idols as ordered by King Nebuchadnezzar. As described by Daniel, "Nebuchadnezzar said to them, 'Is it true, Shadrach, Meshach, and Abednego, that you do not serve my gods or worship the image of gold I have set up? Now when you hear the sound of the horn, flute, zither, lyre, harp, pipe, and all kinds of music, if you are ready to fall down and worship the image I made, very good. But if you do not worship it, you will be thrown immediately into a blazing furnace.'"

They refused.

So, true to his promise, Nebuchadnezzar had the three men tossed into the furnace, which he ordered heated seven times hotter than usual. A curious thing happened next. Nebuchadnezzar looked into the furnace and saw Shadrach, Meshach, and Abednego dancing—along with a fourth man, who was described as looking like "a son of the gods." (Hint: it was Jesus.) Nebuchadnezzar ordered the men out of the furnace and when they appeared he saw "the fire had not harmed their bodies, nor was a hair of their heads singed; their robes were not scorched, and there was no smell of fire on them."

Nebuchadnezzar was so amazed that he then ordered that no harm come to Shadrach, Meshach, and Abednego and he promoted them.

You see, Shadrach, Meshach, and Abednego kept the faith, refused to bow down, looked the threat in the eye, and remained faithful under the pressure, so they were protected and ultimately rewarded.

That is divine protection. That is courage. That is why Goya survived. That is why Goya thrived. And that is why I'm still here.

CHAPTER 3

FATHER (AND MOTHER) KNOWS BEST.

"Your goal in life is salvation."
—Anthony Vincent Unanue

While I can say, without a doubt, saying the word "blessed" at the White House was the explosive catalyst that changed my life for today, and quite frankly, for all of my remaining days, my course was actually determined many years ago, and not by a singular word but rather by a man, the greatest I have ever known—my father, Anthony Vincent Unanue. To further share any part of what's happened in my life would be a pointless exercise if I didn't first share how I came to believe what I believe, why I had the strength of conviction to say, "Hell no, I won't apologize," and why I stand upon an unshakable moral foundation—a foundation laid by the most extraordinary of men.

Dad passed away when he was just forty-eight years old. Leukemia is an awful, horrific disease that steals, kills, and destroys and it takes those we love far too soon. I was twenty-one when Dad died—a kid, really—but fortunately for me, the wisdom he shared and the values he taught put me on a path I believe he'd be pretty proud of.

You may have heard this famous quote of Ralph Waldo Emerson: "It's not the destination. It's the journey." I don't necessarily agree. My destination is Heaven, and that matters a great deal. Although, the journey we're called to take on Earth must be profound for it determines our ultimate destination. Dad taught me that. He always said, "Your goal in life is salvation." Yes, I run a generational family business, but Goya was never the priority in my immediate family when I was growing up—salvation was and is. That was the only way Dad would have it. Truth be told, he never really wanted to be in the family business, he wanted to be a priest, and that's why Dad lived his entire life guided by his religious principles. To this day, my father's (and mother's) faith, unconditional love, and guidance have been, and will be, the greatest influence on my life, my faith, my heart, and my soul.

I grew up in what some people might call a privileged family, but not for the reason one might think. Why was it privileged? Not because of money—we didn't have much of that in the early days, but because I had both a mother and a father. My beautiful mother, Betty, was a stay-at-home mom, which was a real blessing and, to be blunt, a privilege. It's funny because what we had back then is a rarity today. It was much more commonplace in the 1950s for families to have a father who went off to work while the mother stayed home taking care of the home and family. If we had more of that today, both a mother and a father in the home, who knows, maybe we'd be able to fix more of society's ills.

I was born Robert Ignatius Unanue in Teaneck, New Jersey, in March of 1954. My father very much loved the teachings of Saint Ignatius of Loyola, the founder of the Jesuits, so that's why I bear his name. Now, I didn't spend all of my formative years in Teaneck. Because Dad briefly left Goya to work for the federal government, more specifically the Bureau of Ships, which is now known as the Naval Sea Systems Command, we lived for a while in Cheverly, Maryland, a suburb of Washington, DC. Dad was an engineer by training with a degree in electrical engineering and a brilliant mathematician, and although he'd taken this relatively short break from Goya, make no mistake, we Unanues were raised in the family business.

By the time I was ten Dad was once again working for Goya and we were back in Jersey. I recall one Saturday morning in 1964 when he said, "Get dressed, I'm taking you to work." Of course, I was excited! What kid doesn't feel special when their dad takes them to where they work? Besides, I had never been to the plant! So I hurriedly climbed into the front seat of Dad's car and off we went to the Goya plant in the Gowanus neighborhood of Brooklyn, New York. The place was huge, but, of course, when you're ten every place looks huge.

Besides its size, the plant also had a very distinct aroma from the tea leaves we'd imported from Argentina—I still remember the smell. Thank goodness we had the tea because the plant stood next to the Gowanus Canal, and trust me, the tea smelled a whole lot better than the canal! At the time, the canal was so polluted you could almost literally walk on the water. We'd barely arrived at the plant when Dad put me to work doing odd tasks. By the end of the day, I'd become a rich kid—Dad paid me fifty cents for the day's work! That's like five bucks in today's money.

I must have done a good job because Dad brought me back to work when my school's Christmas break came around and for an entire week he had me on the production line. That first full day, which was a Monday, I assembled the calendars we were sending to our customers as Christmas gifts that year. The calendar was a big board adorned with a beautifully printed flamenco dancer. It had a separate packet (sort of like a Post-it notes pad) with each of the 365 days that I had to glue to the board, and then I inserted the entire thing into a big envelope. It was an incredibly classic calendar and, to be honest, a real work of art. I was toiling away for what seemed like hours, and then I looked at the clock. It had been ten minutes! Kids have such a different concept of time, especially when they're doing anything other than playing. The rest of the week I spent working the production line packing olives.

While on the line, a couple of the women working alongside me took me under their wings and would often share their café con leche with me, which they'd pour into an olive oil bottle. Once I took my first sip from that bottle, and the coffee hit my tongue, I was sold. This was the most delicious thing ever! That was my introduction to coffee, and I've enjoyed it ever since, although I do now drink it from a proper coffee cup and not from an olive oil bottle!

That week of work was well worth it; not only was I introduced to the culinary wonder known as café con leche, but

Dad handed me a twenty-dollar bill at the end of the week! Fifty cents an hour, which was big money for a ten-year-old in 1964.

When the school year ended, I spent the entire summer of '65 working at the factory, and I never looked back. I worked at Goya every summer for the next eight years until I graduated from high school. I worked in the warehouse, on the loading dock, on the production line, in the print shop, and in the office. I loaded and drove the Goya trucks. I worked in and learned every facet of the business. I also learned how to be the right kind of person in how I related to people at work. My father taught me the important lesson of always looking at people straight on—never up nor down. He put it like this, "Never look up at anyone nor down at anyone." The relationships I established from very early on at the plant are the basis of the relationships I have today.

A couple of years later, when I was around thirteen, the company expanded our Brooklyn building from two stories to four and placed a giant Goya sign on the roof. For years it served as a sort of beacon for people driving along the Brooklyn-Queens Expressway, more commonly known to New Yorkers as the BQE. I keep a replica of that sign on my office desk in Texas, and you'll often see it whenever I'm interviewed on television. I climbed that giant sign once and was having a blast right up until Dad fired me for it. But after the sufficient amount of time passed for me to learn my lesson, he then rehired me. I never climbed the sign again, although I can't make any guarantees my cousins didn't.

I won't pretend that my father and I had a completely Pollyanna relationship. No father/son relationship is that way. We'd butt heads on occasion, but to me, it's tempering of the metal. Iron sharpens iron. We learn more from our disagreements and failures and become stronger and sharper as a result. Look, I was a kid learning about life and about work from his dad and I had a lot to learn.

I liked working. After all, Dad and Mom did raise me and my five siblings with a strong work ethic. Since we were so deeply rooted in God, family, and work, Mom and Dad obviously also raised us with a spiritual ethic, in a religious environment—a devout Catholic environment. I even served as an altar boy at our local parish church. All of us kids were intensely loved, but beyond work we were also expected to toe the line spiritually.

My parents made sure I got a Catholic school education even though we weren't particularly well off at that time. And if my home provided a pious yet kind and loving environment, my school wasn't exactly that. But you have to consider how society and the approach to education was wildly different fifty to sixty years ago.

When I was in elementary school, there were seventy-one kids in my class with just one instructor watching all of us. One per seventy-one—not exactly a ratio that fosters one-on-one attention. For the educators there, discipline seemed to be paramount. Make sure the kids stay quiet. Make sure they don't talk out of line...that sort of thing. I'm all for discipline but we now know the importance of mental health for young, school-aged children. What about the child who may have been dyslexic? What about the troublemaker who was merely acting out because they had problems at home? Maybe ADHD? How about the disruptive class clown who used humor to mask their pain? These kids fell through the cracks. There were no learning disability teachers or specialists in the classrooms. More than 10 percent of the kids are on the spectrum and they're brilliant people, but you teach them differently. Educators sixty years ago didn't know any better. They didn't address those challenges and weren't as sophisticated as today's educators who would recognize them. But, of course, many of today's educators push woke ideologies on their students. When I was in school, we learned reading, writing, and arithmetic. I am just so grateful that I had wonderful, loving parents to mitigate the emotional challenges of school.

I will say that while the school may have been a product of the times and that's why the teachers weren't necessarily trained to deal with the various mental health challenges of its students, they were outstanding in teaching us in the ways of the faith. We were strong in the *Catechism of the Catholic Church* and could answer just about any faith question a priest posed to us.

That said, I learned so much more about how to be successful in life from my father than I ever did from school. Dad once told me, "Education gives you the freedom to not compromise your values and integrity." Truer words were never spoken. Although when it came to learning about my faith, my Catholic school was obviously invaluable. I learned the importance, not just of faith and of following the rules of the church, but also of serving others. That's why I became an altar boy and why I have a heart for helping people.

As for Dad, as I reference quite frequently, he lived by three values, in this order—God. Family. Work. These are the values that, to this day, guide and govern everything we do at Goya. They're the values upon which this incredible country of ours was built and the same values embraced by Hispanic culture, and the values that help lead to prosperity. Whether it's financial, spiritual, or emotional, prosperity can't be realized without those three things—God. Family. Work. Dad never wavered from those, and he made sure that his six kids didn't either.

CHAPTER 4

DAD V. ROE V. WADE.

"Therefore, my dear brothers and sisters, stand firm. Let nothing move you. Always give your-selves fully to the work of the Lord, because you know that your labor in the Lord is not in vain."

—*1 Corinthians 15:58*

In the aftermath of the "blessed" controversy, as I've mentioned, President Trump told me I had courage for standing up to cancel culture. He told me on the phone and also in a letter that I now have framed in my home office. Trust me, it wasn't easy standing up to the madness. But as another president, Franklin D. Roosevelt, once trumpeted, "Courage is not the absence of fear but rather the assessment that something else is more important than fear." And that's how I felt. How else can you stand firm under the pressure of a nonstop assault on your character and on your business? I assessed that something else was more important than fear.

When you're facing ruination, you don't you buckle. That's courage. The Cowardly Lion in *The Wizard of Oz* put it succinctly and colorfully when he sang about how courage is the secret sauce that made kings out of slaves. It's true. But courage isn't necessarily something you're born with (or provided by a wizard). I was blessed to have lived with the most courageous man I've ever known—my father—who set the example for me and my siblings. And his example could not have been any more profound than it was in 1973 when he took a bold stance on abortion that forever seared into my brain what courage and conviction look like.

As a devout Catholic, Dad was staunchly pro-life—most devout Catholics are. But he was so principled that when the Supreme Court of the United States ruled in favor of protecting abortion in its landmark 1973 decision, Roe v. Wade, my father decided to move our entire family from our home in New Jersey to Spain. He didn't just talk about it, he had us actually leave the country. This man walked the talk. Few people possess that kind of conviction, and in that regard, my father was a giant among men. Contrast what he did with the empty rhetoric you often hear nowadays. How many times did a celebrity back in 2016 say something like, "If Donald Trump wins the election I'm moving to Canada." Yeah, well not a single one of them left the country. Not one. You don't often see the kind of integrity my father had, and clearly no leftist celebrity has any.

The Roe v. Wade ruling and what it meant for the future kept both my father and mother up at night and they spoke about it at length. They thought about it quite fully and Dad's decision to move the family wasn't made flippantly. He didn't just say, "Hey, we're going to Spain."

Besides my mother, Dad spoke with his brothers and his father, Prudencio, the founder of Goya. They agreed with his convictions and the ideas he had about how to expand the business in Spain. After quite a bit of consideration, my father finally decided we had to leave the United States. Had his father and brothers not agreed with him, Dad would have quit Goya and still left the country. We moved in the summer of 1973.

You see, the issue for my father wasn't just abortion; he saw how this was the beginning of the devaluing of life in America. And he proved to be clairvoyant in that regard. We see today how the extreme Left has eliminated any line between the life and the death of an unborn child. At no point do they value the life of a human being. If you ask abortion advocates, a lot of them will tell you how they support killing a baby right up until the time of birth. With ease they'll disregard life—a child killed in an instant. That's where we are today.

Dad saw it coming.

My father valued life at all stages, and his outlook was born from faith. To grasp Dad's faith more fully, we need to go back to 1966—that's when he was diagnosed with leukemia and given two weeks to live. At that time my mother was pregnant with my youngest brother. She was devastated. Though he was given just a couple of weeks, my dad's faith and desire to live, mainly to support his wife and six children, kept him alive for another ten years. Dad wanted to stay alive to not only support us but to guide us in the faith. That's why he was so strong in his convictions and taught us things like, "Your goal in life is salvation," and, "Stay close to the Sacraments." He was 225 pounds when he was diagnosed but just 65 pounds when he died. The disease consumed him but his faith and will were strong.

He was sapped of energy for those ten years. Sometimes he would sneak out to his car and catch a nap at work so as to not raise attention. When Roe v. Wade happened, Dad was understandably upset. He couldn't believe American taxpayers had to basically pay for the decisions made by others to stop a beating heart. As a country, we were not valuing life. Though he was facing death, Dad looked to leave America and was willing to do whatever it took to continue to support his family. He once told us, "You work as a means to live, not live to work."

The decision didn't come as a surprise to our family because Dad made clear for almost a year that he couldn't live in a country that supported abortion and devalued life and he didn't want his tax dollars helping to fund it. This was the example I had—a man who said what he meant and meant what he said and stood up for what he believed despite the cost. That's why, to this day, I am so resolute in my convictions.

When Dad first brought up moving to Spain, my mother wasn't exactly thrilled. Nevertheless, she was a devoted wife and respected Dad's decision despite initially telling him, "I'm not going." God bless my mother, she half-jokingly protested the move repeatedly, right up until we showed up to the airport. Then on the plane to Spain she says, "Okay Tony, well, I'm not going to stay long. I'll be coming right back." She was tough yet supportive, so in the end my father's steadfast conviction won out. We settled into Seville where Dad set up Goya's olive packing plant and olive oil factory.

Building the factory was the easy part—getting the product out of the country, not so much. Dad had several difficulties in getting a license from the Spanish National Olive Syndicate to export the olives, but by jumping through the right hoops, such as having a cousin partner and obtaining Spanish citizenship, after a year, he got the factory up and running. It's funny to think that in 2024 Goya celebrates fifty years in Spain.

This was one of the reasons my grandfather was okay with the move to Spain. The decision wasn't random—it was quite organic, in fact. My father, as had all the members of our family, used to pack olives at our facilities in Brooklyn and Manhattan. He'd often travel to Spain where the olives were grown and from where they were shipped to us. It was during one particular visit overseas when Dad learned that if we packed our olives in Spain rather than in the United States, we'd get some sort of credit. So he said to his father, "I'll go to Spain, pack the olives there, and ship them to the United States so we can avail ourselves of that credit." So, essentially, Dad got to honor his convictions by moving to Spain, and Goya expanded its business interests. Win-win. Although don't misunderstand—while the credit was a bonus, it was not the determining factor in switching our domestic olive and olive oil production to Spain, my father's conviction was. For him, our move to Spain was a journey of faith, conviction, and salvation!

The move was a profound change for all of us—it turned our world upside down, and it certainly wasn't easy. I didn't even speak Spanish. Imagine that. I'd taken three years of Spanish in high school, but it was useless. After graduation, I attended Merrimack College, a small Catholic school of

Augustinian heritage in North Andover, Massachusetts, just north of Boston. I studied accounting there for one year but then left to make the move to Spain. (I did later return and finish the five-year work-study program to earn my degree.) Once we'd arrived in our new country, my father enrolled me in the University of Seville. Let me say, attending school there initially was a real shock. The college experience in Spain wasn't like the college experience in America. First of all, as you know, I didn't speak the language. However, that changed quickly. I learned Spanish in six months. I had no choice, not if I wanted any kind of a productive life in Spain. I like to joke that in Seville you have two language options—you can either speak Spanish or you can speak Spanish. Those are the two options.

We all had to get used to a very different culture. The first thing I noticed was the scale of everything, which was so much smaller than the United States. My brother and I would drive around town in a Seat 850—a tiny Spanish sedan with a rear motor and forty-six horsepower, which was based on the Fiat 850 and popular across Europe in the 1960s and early '70s. We'd cram into the front seat and feel like a couple of circus clowns as we navigated narrow streets in what looked like a toy car. Trust me, the streets of New Jersey were like wide-lane, luxury, comfort cruises compared to some of the streets in Seville.

You have to remember that I was an American teenager. Moving to Spain was a jolt. There I was at nineteen trying to adjust to a new culture in a new country. The simplest things, like what was on television, were now different. In America we take for granted the myriad of program choices we have available with the simple flick of a switch. Spanish television in 1974 was most assuredly not comparable to what I was used to. There were only two stations—one would come on in the morning and the other in the afternoon. That was it. Talk about limited viewing options. It also didn't help that I didn't speak Spanish when we first arrived. I mean, I couldn't understand what was being said on those shows even if I'd wanted to watch them.

What was worse than the cars and the lack of television viewing choices was the heat. I'd just come from New Jersey, where we never experienced temperatures that reached 115 degrees, as they did in Seville, and our new home did not have air conditioning. It was brutal. Oh, and the heat made breakfast fun as well. Every morning we'd drink warm, fresh milk. And by "fresh," I mean, someone would draw it from a cow, put it in a bottle, and deliver it. No refrigeration, pasteurization, or anything else that we take for granted in the United States. Life in Seville was all very new, somewhat rustic, and decidedly different.

My mother also had a hard time adjusting to life in Spain. She wasn't Hispanic, she was Irish American, and didn't speak Spanish. Eleanor Elizabeth isn't exactly a Spanish-sounding name either. Actually, Mom went by "Betty," which is about as Hispanic as "Jane Smith." This made the move to Spain even more difficult for her. Like me, Mom had to adjust to this new way of living. It was all so rudimentary. When she first went to a market Mom was stunned to see whole chickens with the feet still on them. Early on someone handed my mother a gift box, and when she opened it, there inside was a dead rabbit, with its coat and everything. Mom was more than a little freaked out, so much so, she almost went back to America.

My mother truly sacrificed a lot. Spanish wasn't her language nor her culture, and because she wasn't Hispanic, there was a difficult dynamic with Dad's side of the family. Several of his relatives often shunned the two of them. But Dad was devoted to my mother, so how the rest of the family viewed them as a couple made no difference to him. He never had a problem in standing up to anyone in the family. Once, when one of his brothers had consistently been disrespectful and treated him horribly, Dad quit Goya. That was the time when he went to work for the federal government. But as you know, he did later return to the family business.

Abortion, and the devaluing of life, really was an outlier of a bigger issue my father was protesting—that our country was moving away from God. This was not happening in Spain. Spain may not be like this today, but in the early to mid-1970s when we moved there, it was a country that valued and protected life—a country where Dad wanted to live out his life, hopefully with his family by his side.

My father had an incomparable capacity for standing up for what he believed. He proved it not only by choosing to leave the country over the abortion issue and how America was devaluing life but also by protesting having to pay income taxes that year because he didn't want his money helping to destroy even one life. He held off paying in the hopes that he'd hear from the IRS—Dad wanted to fight the government over the issue. But while he was waiting for the fight, one of his brothers paid Dad's taxes without him knowing it. My uncle didn't want Goya involved in a tax protest with the IRS. But Dad would have absolutely fought the government if it had come to that—that's how strongly he felt.

My father was a simple man. He didn't care about money. He didn't care about material possessions. He only cared about living the right kind of life. We weren't rich, yet Dad would sometimes give his entire paycheck to the less fortunate. How incredible is a man who does that? How charitable, unselfish, kind, and giving? This was my example. This is why I don't think twice about sending food to people in need after a disaster or in donating to food banks. My father's example in valuing life and protecting the unborn is also why I have a heart for helping children.

Sadly, Dad didn't get to live out his remaining years in Spain. A couple years after we relocated, we had to move back to the United States so my father could receive medical treatment. Though Dad withered into a near shell of himself physically, spiritually he was as strong as ever. My father had zero problem with death. Zero. He wasn't afraid to die because he knew he had his spiritual ducks in a row and that his destination was Heaven. He used to tell me, "Life is simple. You just have to follow Christ. It's as simple as that. What is there to worry about?"

When Dad was dying he confessed that there were times when he'd be on the way to work and be praying in the car, but then would become distracted by something, and stop praying. He felt bad about that. I believe he shared that with me and my siblings so that we'd all start and end each day in prayer. There were many times working with him in Brooklyn when we would attend noon mass at a nearby church.

Dad did outlive the timeline of what he'd been told in August of 1975. As doctors had done ten years earlier, they again gave him just two days, but he lived for another several months and passed on March 23, 1976, just six days after his father, my grandfather, Prudencio died. As you can imagine, I was utterly devastated. Although, oddly, at the burial, I was overcome, seriously overcome, by a tremendous peace. It's something I'll never forget. I believe this was an incredible gift given to me by the Holy Spirit and my dad. My older sister later told me she felt the same thing. There was a certain joy in knowing that Dad was now at peace and that the Spirit of God, which is love, was enveloping us all with peace. My father's spirit and that peace has accompanied me throughout life and to the Rose Garden...and basically, everywhere I go these days.

After Dad died, I decided to stay in the United States and not return to Spain.

To lose a father at twenty-one—I mean, you're barely an adult. At his funeral, everyone talked about my father's strength of conviction. Dad was my compass, both morally and spiritually, and to lose him caused indescribable pain. My father was everything to me. He was my hero and my mentor, and his death left me with a gaping hole. The loss was intense and there were times not long after Dad passed when I'd dream about him. I still do every now and again.

In my father's absence, my Uncle Frank, though he could never replace my dad, treated me like his own son. He taught me the inner workings of the business and how to navigate the pitfalls one often encounters in running a massive company like Goya. Frank was also there for me on March 21, 1986, when my incredible mother lost her battle with lung cancer, almost ten years to the day after my father passed. Frank himself would pass away in 2002 and I will never, ever forget all the incredible advice he gave on how to be a good executive and a good man, and the comfort he provided when I lost the two most important people in my life.

The Gospel of Luke 12:48 says, "From everyone who has been given much, much will be demanded; and from the one who has been entrusted with much, much more will be asked." My parents gave me much and entrusted me with much. I have a lot to give back. Dad set a very high bar and his standard is not an easy standard to reach. I try but truth be told, I couldn't walk even one step in his shoes. I've always thought my father should be recognized as a saint. He is, hands down, the greatest man I've ever known, and it was his spirit, his convictions, and his tenacity that I carried with me to the White House. I believe my father would want me to use the platform I've been given to spread his message of valuing life. After all, he's why I have the courage to stand by my words and why I'll never back down from trying to do what's right—for me, my family, and my country.

Prophecies,
Miracles, and DJT

CHAPTER 5

LOVE AND BUILD VS. HATE AND DESTROY.

*"Mankind is composed of two sorts of men—
those who love and create, and
those who hate and destroy."*

—*José Martí, Cuban poet and patriot*

If there's anything the Rose Garden experience and the scale of its aftermath made clear to me, it's that there was no human way the reaction could have been so enormous without the hand of God.

There's also a lesson learned about the breadth of the hatred in America.

Each of us has a calling. I believe we are called to value our lives, the lives of others, our families, to have purpose and goodness as individuals, and to love each other. God, in his infinite wisdom, gave us "free will" to do with our lives what we want. Despite being called to love and build, He gave us the freedom to choose to hate and destroy, and sadly that's what's been happening in our country. God created humanity and humanity has created a way to destroy itself. We need to let go of the weapons of hate, division, and war, and embrace completely the power of God and prayer.

I've been growing ever more frustrated by the journey this beautiful country of ours has taken toward values that aren't just counter to the cornerstones of the values my father taught me of God, family, and work, but are decidedly anti-American. Look at what we've allowed to permeate our nation—division, hatred, intolerance of decency, and identity politics that say a man can be a woman, a woman can be a man, and that it's perfectly acceptable to mutilate children and call it "gender-affirming healthcare." These aren't things a true God-fearing country would tolerate.

Our culture has devolved from neighbor helping neighbor to people thinking only of themselves. They "identify" in all manner of ways rather than thinking of others. It's all become so selfish and, to be frank, somewhat narcissistic. As a country what we really need is to love our neighbors, and the world, as ourselves. Jesus called that the second greatest commandment after loving God with all your heart.

It seems half the country has eschewed all decency and morality. And what's worse, people on that side aren't content to ascribe their misguided ideologies solely to their own lives, they're trying to force you to live them too.

How do we fix any of this?

The United States must return to God. He is the answer, but it's our choice as to whether we want to listen. We must let go of hate, embrace love, and fill the divide that widens more with each passing day. For there to be any hope of avoiding the current collision course with socialism, and for all intents and purposes, the total annihilation of decency, freedom, and everything that goes with it, the United States must return to God.

Period.

It won't necessarily be easy. We're in a war between good and evil. Tyrannical politicians no longer hide their intentions. The veil came off with the arrival of the COVID-19 pandemic. The government didn't just shut down businesses, it struck at the core of our faith by also shutting down churches. Religion, more specifically, God, is the foundation on which America was built, yet churches were targeted as though they were houses of ill repute. Pastors, priests, reverends, rabbis, and people from all manner of denomination who dared gather for worship were deemed criminals by the government. The founders of our country, the brave people who'd left England in pursuit of religious liberty, certainly never envisioned something like this. Not here. Land of the free. We had reports of church services held in parking lots, with people in cars by themselves, being ordered by police to disperse or face arrest. It was like 1930s Germany.

What became apparent was the pandemic didn't change the character of the people in charge—it *revealed* it. And unless we address the underlying reasons for why things are changing now, we won't have much of a country in a few years, at least not a free one.

That's why the 2024 presidential election is arguably the most consequential of our lifetime. If it goes the wrong way, America is headed for communism—a system void of human decency, human rights, and, most importantly, of God.

I love America. The Hispanic community loves America. But the America in which we grew up—the America that embraced its solid core values, which gave immigrant families like ours immeasurable opportunity, is on the precipice of extinction. It has forsaken its godly values. America needs a leader who'll champion those values and citizens who'll embrace them.

That leader?

Donald J. Trump.

Admittedly, for some people, this is a stunning claim and not easily digestible. That's where we now are as a society—divided and polarized and incapable of embracing opposing views or critical thought. It's unfortunate, but I get it. Trump was once looked at as the personification of the 1980s' excess, and although he's an extraordinarily successful businessman whose work over the years has revitalized many parts of New York City, he's still relentlessly accused of all manner of unsavory behavior, with the negativity ramping up in 2015, the moment he descended on the escalator at Trump Tower to announce his first candidacy for president. For people who dislike Trump's "America First" ideology he can appear boorish and not quite the quintessence of virtue. Doubters would ask, "This is the guy so pious that God is looking to him to lead an entire nation—a nation gone spiritually astray—to the foot of the cross?"

Yes. Absolutely, yes.

What one must understand is that it's not about the politics. It's not about Trump becoming president. It's about our salvation and the future of this country—the future of the world. Can I say Trump was called by God to lead America back to Him? Yes, I can...and I have. A couple of weeks after the infamous "blessed" Rose Garden news conference, and amid the darkness in the aftermath, I sent then president Trump a handwritten letter, in which I shared just exactly what I believed.

> *"I believe that God has chosen you because of your faith, love of country, courage, and leadership to bring our country closer to Him.*
>
> *I pray for you, Mr. President, your family, and our great nation that you will, not only prevail in this endeavor, but believe that history will recognize you as a great leader of the greatest country on earth."*

Say what you will about the man, but Trump's achievements in terms of religion cannot be argued. Without doubt, they make a compelling case that as president he was in the process of leading America back to God. Among Trump's accomplishments—the first sitting president in history to address the annual March for Life; signed an executive order reinstating the Mexico City Policy, which prevented approximately nine billion dollars of foreign aid from funding abortion worldwide; formed the Conscience and Religious Freedom Division within the US Department of Health and Human Services, which protected religious freedom and kept taxpayer money from being used to discriminate against religion; the first president to meet with the United Nations to call for an end religious persecution; signed the Executive Order on Promoting Free Speech and Religious Liberty during the National Day of Prayer; appointed justices who would later rule to overturn Roe V. Wade and send the issue of abortion back to the states. These are but a smattering of Trump's efforts made in the name of religious freedom and the sanctity of life—values embraced by most Americans and by the hardworking immigrants who came here seeking the American Dream.

Despite what his critics would have you believe, Donald Trump is a man after God's own heart. It's a welcoming stroll down memory lane recalling when he'd post social media video messages on religious holidays. I remember one in particular, on Easter Sunday, "We remember the suffering and death of God's only son and His glorious resurrection on the third day. On Easter Sunday we proclaim with joy, Christ is risen." That's the sort of message we expect from a man of God and one echoed by the majority of American citizens who consider themselves Christian.

Contrast Trump's Easter message with that of Joe Biden, who in 2024, celebrated his religion—woke extremism—by boldly honoring an alternative lifestyle instead of the resurrection of Jesus and proclaiming the Transgender Day of Visibility, which happened to fall on Easter Sunday that year. "On Transgender Day of Visibility, we honor the extraordinary courage and contributions of transgender Americans and reaffirm our Nation's commitment to forming a more perfect Union—where all people are created equal and treated equally throughout their lives," the proclamation said. On the holiest day of the year for Christians, Biden chose to pander to the less than one half of 1 percent of Americans who identify as transgender.[1] What about the extraordinary courage and contributions of Jesus Christ? Shouldn't we honor that or at least respect those who do?

The Transgender Day of Visibility didn't begin with Biden; it began in 2009 during the Obama administration and has been observed on March 31 every year since. In fact, Biden has issued a proclamation for it every year of his presidency. He's the only president to have ever done so.

So why did 2024's proclamation trigger such outrage and sharp rebuke from Christians? The answer is that 2024 was the first year the Transgender Day of Visibility fell on the same day as Easter and Biden chose to continue his relentless assault on Christianity by propping up the radical, "progressive" cause instead. Biden's proclamation was so poorly received that even the highest profile transgendered person ever, Caitlyn Jenner, lambasted him, "I am absolutely disgusted that Joe Biden has declared the most Holy of Holy days—a self-proclaimed devout Catholic—as Transgender Day of Visibility. The only thing you should be declaring on this day is 'HE is Risen.'"

Amen.

Matt Walsh, a pundit from *The Daily Wire*, minced no words in a post on X where he articulated a brutal and scathing rebuttal to Biden's proclamation, "Our 'catholic' president has chosen the highest holiday on the Christian calendar to celebrate transgenderism. This man is a demon." How Biden

---

1   Jody L. Herman, Andrew R. Flores, and Kathryn K. O'Neill, "How Many Adults and Youth Identify as Transgender in the United States?" The Williams Institute, UCLA School of Law, June 2022.

has not been excommunicated from the Catholic Church is in itself a mystery.

Holy Week 2024 vividly illustrated the contrast between the Left and the Right and their respective visions for our country and the difference between Biden and Trump in how they view God. On Holy Thursday, a religious wake was held in Massapequa, New York, for NYPD officer Jonathan Diller, who was shot and killed during a traffic stop by a violent career criminal. Biden did not attend. Instead, he went to a fundraiser with Barack Obama and Hillary Clinton. Do you know who did attend officer Diller's wake? Donald Trump.

On Good Friday, the Biden White House banned religious-themed Easter egg designs from the annual Celebrating National Guard Families art event. Isn't religion the entire reason Easter exists? "Biden is banning religious symbols from Easter celebrations at the White House, while flying the trans flag and declaring Easter Sunday to be 'Trans Visibility Day,'" Donald Trump Jr. reacted in a post on X. "This is the left's new religion. They want people worshiping the trans flag instead of God. They must be stopped."

Meantime, earlier during Holy Week, Donald Trump announced he'd teamed up with country music star Lee Greenwood on a special edition Bible called the "God Bless the USA Bible." The former president has often said the Bible is his favorite book. In a video announcing the special edition posted on his Truth Social platform Trump acutely noted the spiritual void plaguing America, "It's a very sad thing that's happening in our country. But we're going to get it turned around. Religion and Christianity are the biggest things missing from this country and I truly believe that we need to bring them back and we have to bring them back fast. I think it's one of the biggest problems we have. That's why our country is going haywire—we've lost religion in this country." He recognized the brilliance of the Founding Fathers and how they "did a tremendous thing when they built America on Judeo-Christian values."

Trump also vowed to designate November 5th as "Christian Visibility Day" when he wins the presidency in 2024.

My belief in Trump isn't rooted in political conservatism. It's rooted in the prayerful return of the old-school values of which I've spoken so frequently—God. Family. Work. I've mentioned how my father embraced those and how they're the cornerstones of most Hispanic families. What's particularly telling about how Hispanics view Trump is that when polled by the news division of the Spanish-language television network, Univision, half of those surveyed said they planned to vote for Trump over any other GOP presidential hopeful.[2] Despite the politically motivated federal indictments, the poll also showed that Trump's support with Hispanics is higher than when he left office in 2020.

All of this is the hand of God. Think about what Trump has weathered. For the better part of the last decade, he's withstood a malevolent horde working to destroy him. It takes courage to stand up against that relentless assault. Every, single day so-called progressives, militant zealots for socialism, anti-American guerrillas, and the elites of the Washington

---

2   Sergio García-Ríos et al., "Univision Poll: Donald Trump is the favorite among Republican Hispanics, despite his legal troubles," Univision, September 25, 2023.

swamp tell Trump, in both action and words, "We're going to beat you up." "We're going to sue you." "We're going to destroy your business." "We're going to arrest you." "We're going to vilify you." "We're going to falsely accuse you of all manner of crime." "For every waking moment of your life, we'll be working to destroy you." Think about that. Could any average person besieged by this level of relentless persecution continue moving forward? Not without courage, a true love of country and its people, and divine providence.

This is the hand of God.

Our country is under attack, our children are under attack, and "the only thing necessary for the triumph of evil is for good men to do nothing." That's a quote (often incorrectly attributed to Irish philosopher Edmund Burke) dating back to the 1800s which still applies, perhaps now more than ever. In this spiritual war we cannot stand idly by and do nothing. The mission is to bring the country closer to God and He has called His warriors to battle.

America will come back to God and Trump will be the warrior leading it there.

All of the signs and one very bold prediction from a tiny town on the other side of the world point to it.

CHAPTER 6

THE HERMIT OF LORETO.

"The man who, in the future, is going to lead America back to God, is Donald J. Trump."

—Tom Zimmer aka *"The Hermit of Loreto"*

In the summer of 2023, I'd been thinking a lot about a place called The Holy House of Loreto. Many Catholics know it as the home of Mary, where she was born and raised and where, as a teenager, she'd be told by the archangel Gabriel that she was favored by God and would give birth to a son she'd name Jesus. Loreto is a charming enclave about three hours northeast of Rome, on the Musone River, just a few miles off the eastern coast of Italy. On a clear day, if you're so inclined, you can stand just about anywhere and gaze upon the gorgeous turquoise waters of the Adriatic Sea, which extend for as far as the eye can see. Loreto itself is 4700 miles from Washington, DC, but it might as well be on another planet. So, when I heard of a man, an American, who'd left everything he owned and moved to Italy to dedicate himself to praying inside The Holy House of Loreto, and then prophesied about the person who'd lead America back to God, I was more than a bit intrigued.

As most of us know, Mary actually lived in Nazareth, not Italy. But according to tradition, in 1291, as the Muslim army looted the holy places in Israel, Mary's home, for its protection, was transported by angels from Nazareth to a spot in what is now Croatia. (Realistically, the home was likely put on a ship by the Crusaders returning to Europe, although I don't discount that angels can do that sort of thing.) Three years later the house was similarly carried across the Adriatic to Recanati, Italy, and then ultimately transported another five miles to Loreto in 1295. A basilica was built around the Holy House, which is now encased in marble at the center of the basilica. This is one of the holiest sites in Catholicism, and a pilgrimage millions of people have made for more than seven hundred years, and certainly one I'd make regardless of any prophecy.

Before I would venture off to Italy, I'd been marinating on that prophecy—the one about Donald Trump leading America back to God. Why wouldn't I? I've said in countless interviews that for our country to stave off socialism and to have any hope of a successful future, it must return to God. So, I wondered, who was this guy who'd made this prediction?

After a bit of sleuthing, I came upon a video uploaded to YouTube by a priest from Providence, Rhode Island, named Father Giacomo Capoverdi, which he'd put on the platform about a month after Donald Trump was sworn in as president in 2017. At first glance the video seemed innocuous enough. Here was a respectable Catholic priest who'd been on the platform for a year but had yet to post a single video. To this day, it's the only video Father Capoverdi has ever uploaded. In it, he spends roughly eight minutes telling the story of Tom Zimmer, a man better known among Catholics as the "Hermit of Loreto." As described by Father Capoverdi, Zimmer wasn't a priest, nor was he a brother, and he wasn't a particularly "religious" man. But Zimmer was so enamored with The Holy House of Loreto that he left everything behind in America and moved to Loreto to live as a hermit dedicated to prayer. What Father Capoverdi had to say about him was so compelling that the video exploded in popularity—as this book went to press it had nearly eight hundred thousand views.[3]

According to Father Capoverdi, in 1983, in the midst of what's commonly called the "decade of greed," this devout hermit, Zimmer, stood in the Holy House and spoke of a brash New York real estate tycoon and paragon of the decade. "The man who, in the future, is going to lead America back to God is Donald J. Trump," Zimmer prophesied. At the time, to anyone of sound mind, that entire notion seemed as improbable as it was outlandish.

To sort of mitigate the dubiousness of Zimmer's claim, and to lend it some credibility, Father Capoverdi recounted a secondhand conversation Zimmer had with one of Father Capoverdi's friends who tracked him down in the Holy House. According to this friend, Zimmer was apparently so certain that Trump would be the one to lead America back to God that in the same year of his prophecy, Zimmer donated a brick to be put into the Holy Door of Saint Peter's Basilica in

---

3   Giacomo Capoverdi, "Hermit of Loreto," https://www.youtube.com/watch?v=ly-V7kwMRzdo&t=1s, accessed September 5, 2023.

the Vatican with the inscription, "Donald J. Trump." This was thirty-three years *before* Trump would be elected president.

The Holy Door is only opened every 25 years, during a Jubilee or Holy Year as designated by the Pope. In 1983 John Paul II did just that—designated the year a Holy Year—and per tradition, struck the brick wall with a silver hammer and opened it to the pilgrims. Father Capoverdi says the reason Zimmer put the brick in the Holy Door was because he wanted Trump to receive blessings from the masses said in the Vatican.

There's no photograph of that brick, nothing but a hearsay account to prove it's there, and to my knowledge, there's no documented firsthand telling of Zimmer's premonition, so how real is any of this? Outside of God Himself, who knows? Zimmer passed away years ago. But there's one thing that is absolute, unquestionable, and irrefutable—America has strayed dangerously far from God's chosen path and is in dire need of a leader to help get us back to it.

In July of 2023, I scheduled a trip to Italy—not for a pilgrimage to Loreto, at least not initially—but to visit Comunità San Patrignano or, as it's known in English, the San Patrignano Community, in Rimini. It's a drug rehabilitation and recovery community started in 1978. Nearly thirty thousand people have received care there over the years, including the victims of trafficking, and at any given time, roughly 1300 people live on the five-hundred-acre site gratis in exchange for staying clean and helping make the place self-sustaining. As I've mentioned, I started Goya Cares to help the victims of trafficking and to address their mental health, and I've had it on my heart for a while to build a place to give trafficked adults and children an exit back into society. I wanted to see San Patrignano and how it operated, as this amazing place is self-sustaining—up to 65 percent. They make wine, bread, wallpaper, clothing, and other things.

For more than a year, my team and I had been talking about heading over to San Patrignano. With the success of *Sound of Freedom* that summer, we'd decided the timing was perfect for a visit. So we made the arrangements with the people at San Patrignano, scheduled the trip, and went. It was such an inspiration to see the good work they're doing. San Patrignano certainly might end up as a model for what we'd like to build here in America one day.

While we were in Rimini, which is a picturesque and absolutely gorgeous seaside city, we visited a Parmesan cheese factory and a balsamic vinegar factory. I do, after all, run a food company. Then we went up north to magnificent Lake Garda, in the shadow of the Italian Alps. Words cannot adequately describe its majesty or breathtaking beauty. As I stood lakeside, basking in the magnificence of the Italian landscape and the flawlessness of God's handiwork, He gave me a thought, "Wait, where's Loreto? How far is it from here?" I didn't come all this way, to be this close to the home of the Virgin Mary and the place where the Hermit prophesied about Trump, only to leave without seeing it. Though a visit there wasn't on our original agenda, God spoke, and when He speaks, something incredible happens. We left the lake and made our way to Bologna, and when we opened the GPS, it showed Loreto was less than two and a half hours away! So our trip took on a different mission and we made the pilgrimage.

Yet another unplanned gift from God.

Our group piled into the van, I slid behind the wheel, and we hit the road—making our way along Italian highway E45, which morphs into E55, and as we inched closer to Loreto, the seaside view through left side windows captivated us all. Anyone who needs proof God exists need look no further than the Italian coast. Exquisite perfection in nature is never man-made.

The idyllic drive along the Adriatic brought a certain peace and compelled a fair amount of spiritual introspection. The day could not have been more perfect. Then, as it sometimes does, tragedy reared its ugly head and violently changed many lives forever.

As I guided the van along the highway, we were making good time, though I was stuck in the middle lane behind an 18-wheeler. We were rolling along when I spotted a police car with its lights flashing up ahead and to the right. I could only assume the officer was motioning for a car to pull over. "Some poor guy must be getting a ticket," I thought as I instinctively lifted my foot from the gas pedal. Then, in what felt like a nanosecond, a car in the far left lane darted to the right, across the highway, and in front of the 18-wheeler (which was still directly in front of us). What happened next is something I won't soon forget—if ever.

In one horrific moment, the 18-wheeler, which was cruising at what looked like max speed, obliterated that car. It was an explosion of tires and steel with debris launched in every direction. The car disintegrated instantly. The loud sound of metal on metal was just so awful. This was like something you might see in an action movie, but it was all real and happening quite literally in front of us. The people in that car never stood a chance.

The group and I prayed for all of the victims and their families, and we gave thanks to God for our safety. We'd narrowly avoided being caught up in the collision. I'd love to think it was due to my driving skills, after all I did once have a commercial driver's license and would drive the big delivery rigs during my early days at Goya, but I knew, as we all did, that it was God's divine protection.

His hand kept us out of harm's way.

Once we'd made our way through the mayhem on E55 and pondered everything that had happened, it wasn't long before we were rolling down Via Don Giovanni Minzoni, the road alongside the outer walls of the Santuario della Santa Casa di Loreto, also known as The Sanctuary of the Holy House of Loreto.

We'd made it!

I parked our van and as our good fortune would have it, there weren't a lot of people around. Oh, there were a couple tour buses flanking the complex, which appeared to us almost as a mini version of Vatican City—their layouts are very similar—and we found the charming strip of restaurants, cafes, and small boutique hotels outside the brick walls, which you'd typically see buzzing with tourists from all over the world, to be quite peaceful. It was much quainter than when you go to some of these places and the queue to get in is like two hours.

We walked toward the main plaza, and along with the rest of the faithful and the curious who were there, we were greeted by the Monumento a Giovanni Paolo II—the Monument to John Paul II, which stands outside the walls of the complex. The presence of Saint John Paul II is felt everywhere across Europe and I believe he is the greatest pope in the history of the church. As a Catholic, this was as amazing a day as any I could ever have prayed for.

When I stepped into the basilica itself, it was as resplendent as I'd imagined it would be. The aura of its holiness and its splendor commands reverence from everyone who enters regardless of their religion.

The Holy House truly is amazing, so much so that I had no choice but to slyly snap a few pictures and some video on my phone as I walked through it. You're almost compelled to do it—this was the home of Mary, the Blessed Mother. I'm certainly not the first, and definitely not the last, to grab some memories on a smartphone camera.

Positioned on the outside of the Holy House but inside the basilica is an urn, basically a hard, clear plastic box, where visitors can submit a prayer intention, which, in its simplest form, is something, or someone, you want prayed for during Mass. The box must've been five feet tall to accommodate all of the intentions dropped into it. I submitted one that read if the Zimmer prediction was true—that Donald Trump was called to lead America closer to God—that God would make it happen. I did ask several people throughout the basilica whether they'd ever heard of Zimmer, and though he wasn't well known, they did know of him—the fabled Hermit of Loreto, or as they more commonly refer to him, "L'Americano."

Did Zimmer truly prophesy about Donald Trump? I believe he did, and I do know I've never seen a leader move so many people—one who elicits such kinetic energy that it electrifies stadiums filled to capacity—and the overflow crowds outside as Trump does. He is as compelling and charismatic a person as you'll ever see. In my experience, he's also warm-hearted, generous, respectful, and mindful of what others want and need. To be clear, Zimmer never claimed Trump would be president, just that he'd lead America back to God. It's not out of the question, Trump is much more spiritual than people give him credit for. He was guided in his faith early in life by his mother, Mary, who raised him in the Presbyterian church. In fact, when President Trump took the oath of office at his inauguration in 2017, he had his hand on the very Bible his mother gave him when he was nine years old when he'd graduated from Sunday Church Primary School in New York. The former president has often referred to the Bible as his favorite book.

Donald Trump sees what my father saw in 1973—the same thing I now see—that America has fallen victim to a sort of insane, moral anarchy. From technology to academia to media to anti-American politicians, the tearing down of morality in the name of "progress" has pulled this country from its foundation and helped to raise up the woke, the entitled, the lazy, the hateful, and the divisive.

God has issued a mandate for spiritual revival in the United States, not just for Latinos like me, but for all Americans.

For America's sake, we should pray the Hermit was right.

Signs and Wonders…
and Rosaries

CHAPTER 7

UKRAINE, RUSSIA, AND AN UNLIKELY MEETING.

"If you can't feed a hundred people, then feed just one."

—*Mother Teresa*

The people of Ukraine needed hope (and food) in spades in the spring of 2022. About a month after Russian troops came across their border, Ukrainian men, women, and children were running for their lives. This was the biggest military escalation of the Russia/Ukraine conflict since it began in 2014 (although it was quiet during the Trump presidency). In fact, I believe wholeheartedly this never would have happened if Trump had still been president, because when he was president, we had no new wars. None. But, regardless of the politics of who was to blame for this escalation, Ukrainian civilians couldn't get out fast enough. They took off with the clothes on their backs and whatever they could carry. Anyone with even a passing knowledge of that part of the world knows it's not like America—there are no Cracker Barrels, Love's Travel Stops, or convenience stores ubiquitously lining the exits of their highways. So these people were hungry and hurting in a big way.

Whenever there's a humanitarian emergency, regardless of where in the world it is, Goya answers the call to help. We're fortunate in that we're not limited to feeding just one person, we can, and do, feed millions more. Through our Goya Gives initiative we often lead in disaster relief efforts and provide food donations in times of crisis and this situation in Ukraine was definitely a crisis. It was a historic attack and a genocide on innocent civilians, and we couldn't sit back and do nothing. The escalation caused such a mad rush at the stores that there literally was no food in Ukraine.

I watched the news in horror—empty store shelves and desperate people pouring out of Ukraine, with nothing, and nowhere to go. My heart ached for them. I'd begun thinking about how we could help when I got a call from Ivanka Trump. She'd been working with Paula White-Cain, the renowned minister, pastor, and author, and they, too, saw the need to feed those people escaping Ukraine. Ivanka told me how she and Paula hoped to send a million meals over there but weren't sure how to go about it. Quite frankly, that was a huge number, and you can't just load up a truck, show up, and say, "Here's the food, help yourselves." The process of relief, especially international relief, can often be a mind-numbingly futile (and sometimes dangerous) bureaucratic nightmare.

Wanting to help people is the easy part. The hard part is getting the food there. For example, during the early days of the COVID-19 pandemic, we sent nearly a quarter million pounds of food to Venezuela, which used to be one of the world's richest countries but since transitioning into socialism is now one of the most destitute. It's also rife with corruption. To get our food into Venezuela was like something from a 1970s spy thriller. President Nicolás Maduro didn't want any help and wouldn't accept the food. So we had to go in stealth through local groups and the Catholic Church, under the radar so to speak, through certain generals, who all wanted payoffs, and truthfully, I don't know if the food ever made it to the people who really needed it. I pray it did. Can you imagine having to pay someone to accept food? No matter, even when the world is in chaos, Goya tries to do the right thing for people in need. So we made every humanly possible effort to get that food to them.

Fortunately, there wasn't any violence directed toward us in Venezuela, not like there'd been in Haiti a decade earlier. After a horrific 7.0 magnitude earthquake devastated the island, we brought in more than three hundred thousand pounds of food that we'd loaded onto a massive truck at our distribution facility in the Dominican Republic. No sooner had the truck crossed the border into Haiti when it was hijacked by armed gang members who threatened to kill the driver and burn the truck if we didn't give them the food. So our driver did as he was told. Understandable. The food was taken by the gangs who currently run the country.

Again, wanting to help is the easy part, but the delivery— not so much.

These sorts of challenges never stop us though. Feeding and helping people is our mission. We call ourselves La Gran Familia Goya because, as the phrase says, we are a family. But we're not just a family of people from all walks of life and all communities in the Latino world, we're also part of a greater community—the family of the United States and the world. Family is so important—it's the second part of the value system most Hispanics are taught from birth—God, family, and work. The Goya family values community and takes its role within it seriously. When I lived in Puerto Rico early in my career, I remember my Uncle Frank and I sitting down anytime there'd be a natural disaster and talking about how Goya could be of help. We consider it a vital part of what we're called to do.

For Ukraine, I determined that the European arm of our company, Goya Europa, was perfectly positioned to help. We were blessed to have a presence nearby and nimble enough to mobilize products to where they needed to go. Goya Europa has facilities in Madrid and Barcelona, as well as a Goya España factory in Seville, and distribution partners across Europe, all of which would be assets in this endeavor.

My oldest son runs Goya Europa, so I gave him a call. He's a lot like his dad, so naturally he shared my concerns for those people and wanted to do everything he could to help feed them. All of my six children are like that. We saw there'd been a mass arrival of refugees at the border of Ukraine and Poland, so we knew that's where the initial shipment of food had to go.

Our team began handling the logistics of sending the food through our distribution partners in both Ukraine and Poland. Among them, we worked diligently with an amazing organization called Global Empowerment Mission (GEM) and our first shipment from their distribution headquarters in Rzeszów, Poland, was enormous. It weighed in at a whopping 235 metric tons—more than a half million pounds. GEM, and its founder, a Miami philanthropist named Michael Capponi, have done extraordinary work in helping people worldwide get what they need in times of crisis, and they were invaluable to those Ukrainian refugees.

Those incredible people at GEM worked like machines to get the food out. At the Rzeszów distribution facility, pallet upon pallet of Goya products and products from other GEM partners were loaded onto the limited number of semitrucks and buses they had available and driven daily about sixty miles southeast to the village of Medyka, Poland, on the border with Ukraine.

During normal times, Medyka is picturesque and quaint with fewer than three thousand close-knit people living there. But these weren't normal times, and that village simply wasn't equipped to deal with the arrival of literally millions of people, all of whom were in desperate need, without a global relief effort. One of those people was an older woman named Nadia who walked 370 miles from Kyiv to Medyka, carrying just one bag and her cat. Think about that and what it says about the dire circumstances and the desperation. This woman *walked* nearly four hundred miles. GEM shared Nadia's story on its social media accounts, and the good news is she got a ride and made it safely to her friend's home about eight hours north in Gdańsk. Many others weren't as fortunate.

Once the word got out about what Goya was doing to feed those Ukrainian refugees, I got calls from the booking producers working for the various cable news networks, and, of course, from Fox News who asked me to appear on *Fox & Friends*. Since 2020, I've been invited on to Fox News programs so often that sometimes it feels as though I've become old friends with their producers. Of course, I agreed. This was God, once again, providing me a platform upon which to share His message and I wasn't about to waste it. He's the reason I get those invitations at all.

By the way, one thing you might not be aware of, rarely am I ever in an actual studio when I'm on these shows. My segments are almost always either from my office or home, a local studio where there's one camera and a chair positioned in front of a backdrop of a cityscape, or, as in this case, from the warehouse of our manufacturing and distribution facility in Brookshire, Texas.

Ainsley Earhardt, *Fox & Friends'* longtime cohost—a tremendous journalist and wonderful Christian woman—introduced the segment and thanked me for what Goya was doing to feed the Ukrainian refugees. The first thing that came to my mind wasn't food though, instead it was how elections have consequences and what a mess the world had become in the past year. (Joe Biden had become president the year before.) A lot of people might not know how profoundly the decisions made in Washington (or Moscow) affect the food supply or how the conflict between Ukraine and Russia hurt it as well.

At that time, we had two wars in play. Actually, we still do. One, the Biden administration's war on fossil fuels sent inflation skyrocketing and we were pacing 13 percent per month in our foods. Fuel costs went through the roof which, of course, had an adverse effect on the overall cost of transportation. Food has to be delivered by road and rail and that takes fossil fuel. Raise its price and do the math—the cost of everything, including food, rises with it. The pandemic and its related supply chain issues were also a huge contributor to rising costs.

The second war was, of course, the one in Ukraine—a country that makes fertilizer and grows corn and wheat. Russia is also one of the world's biggest exporters of fertilizers. Those two countries control 50 percent of the world's fertilizer and make up nearly a third of global wheat exports and roughly 20 percent of the world's supply of corn. They also have two and a half million acres of sunflowers that are used for cooking oil. So naturally those oil costs went through the roof. In addition, Ukraine and Russia account for a vast amount of the sand used to make glass, which is used for all manner of containers. It's easy to see how the conflict greatly impacted the food supply, the glass supply, the oil supply, and the fertilizer supply, much more than any person not in the food industry might realize.

This was the conversation I was having with Ainsley when what happened in the Rose Garden in 2020 happened again—it happens quite often in fact—I was touched by the Holy Spirit. He led my mind elsewhere and now food was no longer the topic of conversation—it was something much, much bigger, and the reason why I believe I have a platform at all. "The biggest problem Ainsley is that we are moving away from God," I told her and, of course, the millions of people watching. "We need to move closer to God, to value life." There was no stopping me. As I stood in our warehouse, before the giant American flag we'd hung for that canceled Trump visit, God had a message, and I was delivering it. We were calling for faith and a return to God in the midst of war. "With all of the great people in the world, there is hope that all the good can overcome all the evil in the world…and we need to be those beacons of light." In war, whether physical or spiritual, we have two distinct choices—love, build, and unite or hate, divide, and destroy. We must love our neighbor as we love ourselves…it's the only solution to what ails America— and the world. And that's the message I'd hoped to convey as I spoke with Ainsley.

You know, it always amazes me how we say things and never know in those moments just exactly how, if at all, the things we say might be impacting someone else, and why we were compelled to say them. What I didn't know as I stood there on Fox News speaking to millions of people, was that one of them, a woman in Texas, just 160 miles from where I was standing, was so moved by what I'd said about God, she felt compelled to reach out to me—a simple act that led to one of the most profound miracles I'd ever be blessed to witness.

CHAPTER 8

THE MIRACLE OF
THE ROSARIES.

*"He performs wonders that cannot be fath-
omed, miracles that cannot be counted."*

—*Job 5:9*

The signs, wonders, and opportunities God makes available when you're obedient to His voice transcend whatever mere mortals can comprehend or conjure to thought.
I've witnessed many of them firsthand in my own life since
that moment in 2020, when the Holy Spirit placed the word
"blessed" upon my lips at the White House. It's an extraordinary thing to see the hand of God in your life, and on some
days, things happen that seem too good to be true, but if you
have faith, you know they're not. God can never be limited;
He makes things happen you could never make happen on
your own. That's what happened when God opened the door
for me and my team to bring tangible hope, in the form of
rosaries, to the people of war-torn Ukraine.

For the uninitiated in the Catholic faith, prayers of the
rosary are an invaluable part of a believer's spiritual life. The
practice dates back to 1214 when, according to tradition,

the Virgin Mary appeared to Saint Dominic de Guzman in a vision, gave him a rosary, and told him to encourage others to pray it in the hopes of reconciling themselves with God. Each bead represents an individual prayer, and the person praying typically moves their hands from bead to bead as they pray each prayer. The word "rosary" itself comes from Latin, which translated means, "crown of roses." If there ever was a group of people worthy of a crown of roses or basically, this kind of frequent and fervent prayer, it was the Ukrainian refugees…and those holding on to hope they'd survive the Russian offensive. They needed a miracle, and one was headed their way.

After I'd spoken on *Fox & Friends* about the world's need to return to God, things began unfolding rapidly toward what I affectionately call "The Miracle of the Rosaries." To this day, I remain in awe at how God brings people together for His purpose and supplies the things people need when they're at their most despondent.

The day after my television appearance with Ainsley Earhardt, my phone rang—on the other end was Goya's director of public relations for Texas—Mayte Sera Weitzman. Goya is involved in so many community-related initiatives it's not an understatement to say Mayte and I have spoken too many times to count. But this call—this call, I could tell was different.

Mayte told me that a woman in San Antonio named Shannon Haase contacted her after seeing me on Fox News. She went on about how this woman, Shannon, was so impressed that a CEO would speak about God on television that she wanted to know if I would accept a rosary she'd made.

Of course, I would! I was so very touched and honored that someone would consider me in that way. I'm simply a vessel for God's word and was truly humbled by Shannon's selfless gesture. A couple of days later, it arrived—a woven rosary, in blue and white, the same colors as Mother Teresa's iconic sari.

Of course, to anyone who's ever met Shannon, it won't come as a surprise she didn't stop there—with the one rosary. She's as devout and as bold for God as it gets. One rosary would not be enough.

Unknown to us initially, Shannon and a few of her fellow parishioners at the Our Lady of Guadalupe Church, on San Antonio's west side, had launched a mammoth effort to collect rosaries from around the country for Ukraine. They'd gotten too many to count and wanted to give them to us. Why us? We'd soon find out.

I hadn't committed to visiting San Antonio until one morning, a couple of days later, Mayte and I were in my office with the news on the television in the background, when we saw a story that Russia had bombed an art school in Mariupol, Ukraine, with four hundred civilians inside. I sat there, mouth open, disgusted by the true, unmitigated evil on display in 4K color. I took about ten seconds before I looked at Mayte and said, "We have to go to San Antonio and get those rosaries." Mayte immediately texted Shannon, "We're on the way to pick them up!"

Almost immediately Mayte and I climbed into a Goya van and drove over to San Antonio—it's an easy drive on Interstate 10, just a couple of hours west of our facility in Brookshire. As a fun, added bonus, since those vans are so colorfully wrapped with our company logo, Goya would have a mobile billboard cruising along one of Texas's busiest highways!

When we rolled into town, Mayte and I met Shannon at her home and were absolutely blown away by what we saw. First, we were greeted by a roomful of men and women singing hymns—all wonderful people with a sincere love in their eyes that revealed their total devotion to the Lord. Then, there in the middle of a simple, yet now crowded living room was a statue of the Virgin Mary, and at her feet were at least a dozen US Postal Service boxes Shannon and her colleagues had packed with the scores of rosaries they'd made and collected along with cards adorned with an illustration of Our Lady of Guadalupe. I couldn't believe my eyes.

What began as a gesture with one rosary had now become a gesture with thousands. Shannon then unselfishly handed those rosaries over to Mayte and me but made one request as she did, one that for any ordinary person would seem insane, "Take these rosaries to the people of Ukraine!"

Wait, what?

Did Shannon really just say what I think she said? Incredibly, Shannon asked us to carry boxes of rosaries to Ukraine—a huge and seemingly impossible ask. Even more incredibly, I agreed. Why in the world would I do that? Was *I* insane? I'd just agreed to personally take boxes of rosaries to a country currently in a military conflict with Russia. What was I thinking? I mean, a woman who I'd never met before asks me to take rosaries to Ukraine. Sure, why not? I have nothing else to do. I suppose I was caught up in the moment, but truth be told, I had no idea how to get these things into a war-torn country, much less how to distribute them. No international shipping company was delivering into Ukraine, and that's why somebody, more specifically, me, would have to hand-deliver them.

For the record, let me say, Shannon is a special person. She works as an oncology nurse, which is an extraordinary profession. People in the medical field have a gift of bringing healing and hope to so many, yet Shannon has such humility she doesn't brag about the lifesaving work she does. It's her actions, things like handcrafting rosaries in her spare time, that reveal Shannon's profound devotion to God. Clearly, she felt a divine compulsion to request the rosaries be taken to Ukraine. She'd later say, "The prayer in my heart came, 'Ask him, [Bob] if he's going to send food [to Ukraine], will he send the rosaries over to the Ukrainian people?'" So she did. That was nothing short of pure obedience to the voice of the Holy Spirit. Sometimes, the more insane and impossible the ask, the greater the opportunity for God to reveal Himself and His power. And to think all of this happened because I'd spoken about God on television and Shannon happened to be watching. You had to admire her devotion and boldness.

Since I agreed to do it, I was now in a somewhat sticky situation. If I was going to get these rosaries to Ukraine, I would need all the help I could get, both earthly and heavenly. So, before Mayte and I left San Antonio, Shannon and her people arranged for the rosaries to be blessed by the highest possible authority in the church, well, locally anyway—someone they knew well—the archbishop of San Antonio, the Most Reverend Gustavo García-Siller.

Shannon told us, "When you head out, stop by the archbishop's home, he knows you're coming." So we did. When we arrived, Archbishop García-Siller came out, and right there in the driveway, sprinkled holy water on the rosaries, prayed over them, and prayed for us. Then we were on our way back to Brookshire.

By the time Mayte and I got back to Brookshire it was one o'clock in the morning and we were both exhausted and yet exhilarated. It was in this moment we knew without doubt we were in the midst of a miracle. We heard from Shannon again and learned rosaries had been pouring in from around the United States, including about a thousand from my own parish of Saint Faustina in Fulshear, Texas. News of what Shannon and her colleagues were doing was spreading like wildfire, and I'm not sure how or why, other than by the divine intervention of the Holy Spirit.

Mayte and I carried the boxes of rosaries into my office and as we were going through them to try to calculate just how many we had, all of a sudden Mayte excitedly called out, "Bob, look at this!" and held up a medal of the Holy Spirit. If we needed yet another sign that this entire endeavor was orchestrated by God, we certainly got one. I told Mayte that I wanted to keep that medal and take it with us to protect us on our journey.

To this day, I proudly wear that medal around my neck.

As we were ramping up for the journey to Ukraine, I was interviewed for local television newscasts in Houston, as was Shannon, and both Shannon and I were interviewed by Rachel Campos-Duffy—another wonderful journalist and

Christian—on a Saturday edition of *Fox & Friends Weekend*. Shannon projected such spirituality, and she was quite literally glowing, like an angel, and radiating through the screen. Rachel mentioned how the prayer of the rosary was her favorite and asked Shannon how all of this came about, and her answer was short, succinct, and about as powerful as it gets— "The Holy Spirit."

Because Shannon obeyed the voice of the Holy Spirit who very specifically told her, "Ask him [me], if he's going to send food, will he send the rosaries over to the Ukrainian people?" She went from seeing me on television, to making a phone call to Mayte, to sending me one rosary, to receiving thousands more, to inviting Mayte and me into her home, to asking me to take the rosaries to Ukraine, to appearing on Fox News, to me actually going overseas with the rosaries—all within a span of ten days.

Ten days.

There is no earthly way that could ever happen. Ever.

If there was any doubt that God was in the middle of all this, consider the ease and swiftness of how it came together. Within a week and a half after finally meeting Shannon face to face, I was packed for Poland and set to deliver rosaries and the prints of Our Lady of Guadalupe to the Ukrainian refugees on the Poland/Ukraine border. Oh, and the number of rosaries had ballooned from the original one to more than fifteen thousand!

Fifteen thousand! (With tens of thousands more still to come.)

The day I left for Poland, we heard Pope Francis would be consecrating Russia and Ukraine to the Immaculate Heart of Mary, which essentially was him putting his trust in Mary to bring peace, not just to Ukraine, but around the world. I knew then more than ever that I had an even more profound mission. As I told Rachel on Fox News, I believed the rosaries were a source of prayer and love, and the greatest weapon against evil. We packed those fifteen thousand rosaries and prints into several suitcases and I jetted off to Poland...by way of Spain.

Before I'd arrived at the George Bush Intercontinental Airport, I thought the twelve-hour journey from Houston to Newark to Madrid might be a welcome respite from my increasingly hectic schedule, but I was wrong. Even as I'd boarded, walking down the jetway and crossing the threshold through the cabin door, I was consumed by one thought on this flight—the miracle God was performing. Sitting there in the cabin of the Boeing 767, the ever-present hum of the engines wasn't enough to disrupt my thinking on just how all of this happened.

After a layover, the plane made its way out of Newark and was now in full stride over the Atlantic headed for Spain. I sighed and tried to make myself comfortable—at least as comfortable as anyone can get in a bed unfolded from a business class airplane seat—but I couldn't get my mind off those rosaries and the Ukrainian refugees. I was nervous and excited all at the same time.

The journey to Madrid had been a necessary reroute in the interest of time. I'd only scheduled six days for this trip, and

I couldn't waste even one minute of it. Even though we were already two years into the pandemic, US citizens who'd not been injected with one of the COVID-19 vaccines (I was one of them) were being forced to quarantine for seven days upon arrival in Poland. I didn't have that kind of time. I couldn't very well quarantine for seven days when my entire trip was scheduled for six. So, instead of flying directly to Poland, I flew into Madrid, took a PCR test, and when it came back negative, flew into Warsaw with my Spanish passport (I have dual citizenship). Since I was a citizen of the European Union, when I subsequently flew into Poland, no quarantine was required.

When I landed in Warsaw, I met up with Mayte, Syddia, and the rest of the team, who were already there. Unlike me, they *were* vaccinated and could enter Poland without having to be quarantined. We all then traveled by van to Rzeszów— and by "we" I mean me, the team, and the suitcases stuffed with fifteen thousand rosaries and the prints. We were met in Rzeszów by our good friend Michael Capponi, who took us over to the GEM warehouse where we spent the first couple days. From there we jumped into a truck and drove down to Medyka.

Typically it takes a little less than an hour and a half through gorgeous, rolling countryside to get to Medyka from the GEM warehouse. On the way, we even passed a roadside McDonald's as we drove through Przemyśl, which kind of caught me off guard a bit. In America it's not that big of a deal, but the Golden Arches aren't necessarily what you'd expect to see while on a relief mission in a foreign country. In any case, it wasn't long before we turned from National Road

28 onto the main road into the village—the aptly named Główna, which translated into English means "Main."

Driving down Main, as we passed by nondescript houses and a multitude of displaced people, a chaotic scene to be sure, I had but two thoughts—just how was I going to distribute all these rosaries here in Poland, and what incredible miracle would the Holy Spirit perform next?

CHAPTER 9

BLESSINGS (AND ROSARIES) IN UNLIMITED SUPPLY.

"The Holy Rosary is the best artillery
against demons and their followers."

—*Saint Dominic de Guzman*

Before we'd left for Poland, Shannon told Rachel Campos-Duffy how one of the things she hoped would come out of this campaign was that people would pray and "God would take his [Putin's] heart and make it soft—make it a heart of love so the hardened sinners will all of a sudden be resolved and we will have peace." I so appreciated her response because as I've said countless times, love conquers all. It's the greatest weapon against evil and in moving nations toward God.

Even though I concurred with what Rachel told Shannon, "All things are possible with God," until Putin's heart was actually softened, I still had a mission at hand with those thousands of rosaries. A rosary is a prayer and those Ukrainian refugees most assuredly needed prayers.

Once we arrived in Medyka, I walked out among the Ukrainians in the village. The place was an absolute madhouse—thousands of people pouring across the border in buses and media crews everywhere. To be honest, it looked like an end of times nightmare. Thousands of cots were spread out in makeshift shelters and the people sitting on them simply looked defeated. To see the hurt, the discouragement, and the sheer sadness in their faces—it was just so heartbreaking, and yet here I was with thousands of rosaries unsure of what to do. As with food distribution you can't just show up and yell, "Okay here it is, come and get it!"

So what did the team and I do? Well, we just started handing out the rosaries indiscriminately and, really, without any kind of plan. "Hello, God bless you." "Please accept this as a symbol of hope." "We're praying for you, and we love you." "I pray this rosary brings you comfort." Every rosary was different—rope rosaries, bead rosaries, and in all assortments of color. They were the gifts of faith, prayer, and love—the only things that will allow us to survive in the coming days. These people needed all of those things and more. What began as a collaborative mission between Goya Foods and GEM to feed the hungry was now much, much bigger. We were bringing nourishment for souls. But trust me, we definitely never forgot their need for food. After all, GEM did distribute nearly half a million pounds on that first run.

The thing is, we were a very small team, only a handful of people, and we had literally thousands of rosaries to give out. Admittedly, our distribution was all a bit haphazard—and although I knew we were being led by God, we really needed to figure out a proper, more efficient way to get those rosaries to the people who wanted them.

Fortunately, before I'd left home, I called my son who's the general manager of Goya's Texas operation. As good fortune would have it, he had a friend whose father knew someone at the Knights of Columbus (KOC) and they put us in touch with Syzmon Czyszek, KOC's director for international growth in Europe. Amazingly, and this could only come from God, while we were trying to figure out what to do with the rosaries, Syzmon introduced us to a priest of the Dominican order named Father Jon Kalisch who received an urgent note from the Dominican priests embedded in L'viv, Ukraine, asking for, nay, *begging* for rosaries. "We need rosaries! Please get your hands on some! Send them immediately!" Well, we had rosaries—fifteen thousand of them!

How was I going to get any of those rosaries down there though? I wanted to go down and deliver them myself, but I'd been told that if I crossed the border into Ukraine, I'd likely never get out. However, God had already provided a way. As the Gospel according to Saint Matthew says, "Your Father knows what you need before you ask him." We had a need, and He knew it. Turns out our contacts at GEM had three friends who were former United States Army Green Berets—some real tough dudes—who worked for Aerial Recovery, which is basically a humanitarian special ops team that responds to natural and man-made disasters, fights sex trafficking, and tackles some of the most difficult rescue and response missions around the world. These three guys agreed to do us a huge favor, while still performing their own rescue duties in Ukraine. They came and picked up eight thousand rosaries, carried them across the border, and hand-delivered them to the Dominican priests in L'viv.

Once again, God provided.

Honestly, how does this happen without God? It doesn't. And to think almost all of this came about because one person in San Antonio, Texas, heard the voice of the Holy Spirit and was obedient to His voice.

Also, stop and consider the significance of that request from the priests in L'viv—they were of the Dominican Order. The Dominican Order is named for Saint Dominic de Guzman, the one who received the rosary from the Blessed Mother to begin with back in 1214. Coincidence? I don't think so! When you're a true believer, there are no coincidences.

Who says miracles don't happen anymore?

We still had the rest of the rosaries to hand out. But where though? Syzmon gave us the locations KOC deemed most in need, starting with the GEM warehouse in Rzeszów. We left some rosaries for the truck drivers there, for two primary reasons—so they'd have some to give away, and, most importantly, so God would protect them as they made their deliveries.

Next was Medyka. As you now know, we didn't have much of a plan there. We'd walk up to total strangers, chat, and hand them a rosary. But while we were there we were invited by the KOC to visit the third location on their list—the "mercy huts" they'd set up in the border town of Hrebenne, which was a couple of hours away. The huts aren't actual huts, they're really just tents—huge, rigid tents—that look more like buildings. They're incredible. The mercy huts served a profound purpose—they were the hub where refugees could receive immediate aid, which included shelter, food, medical supplies, and clothes. Keep in mind, many of those refugees escaped Ukraine with only the clothes on their backs. Inside the tents you'd find a chapel, priests, nuns, believers, nonbelievers, atheists, and all manner of people in dire straits. The mercy huts provided them all with hope when it seemed there was none. And it gave me hope to see people from all backgrounds loving and contributing.

After spending the day in Medyka, we decided to head back to our hotel in Rzeszów for the night and leave for Hrebenne in the morning. Though the five of us who'd made the trip from the United States were absolutely exhausted, we were so full of spiritual energy we could barely sleep.

Morning came and we loaded into the van and made the two-hour drive to Hrebenne, which is about sixty miles northeast of Medyka, and also right there on the border with Ukraine. It's difficult to put into words what we saw there in Hrebenne. It's easy to watch the news in America, see the images coming out of Ukraine and the Polish border, and think you have a good idea of what's happening. Trust me, television cannot capture the sheer chaos or the horror of what's happening on the ground. While we were in Hrebenne we could hear the nonstop sirens warning of potentially incoming bombs. That made everything incredibly real—something television news could never do. We could also hear shelling from every direction, and seemingly very close—easily within fifteen miles, maybe less. We'd see worried women and children in abject terror wandering aimlessly with stunned looks on their faces. Most of them left husbands, brothers, and older sons behind—good men who wanted to stay and fight for the independence and freedom of their country.

One of those women was a refugee named Nella who was travelling with her six-year-old son. We got to talking and she told me that her husband, along with the other adult men in Ukraine, was required to stay and defend the country. So he'd send his family to safety but not to go with them. I asked Nella, "How did you guys separate? That must've been heartbreaking." With a tear in her eye, Nella shared what her husband told her as she was desperately trying to reconcile their being apart, "Nella," he said, "love and protect our son and I will protect and defend our country and our home."

I saw thousands of women and children in Hrebenne and in Medyka, each of them with stories not unlike Nella's. We attended Holy Mass inside one of the mercy huts to pray for the safe passage of the refugees and for the peace of God to fill the region and end the conflict. Prayer is so vital to survival that even after we'd left Hrebenne, the archbishop of New York, Cardinal Timothy Dolan, made the trip to Poland himself and traveled to Hrebenne to meet the refugees and say Holy Mass for them in that same mercy hut.

One could look at the situation in Ukraine and think a missile fired into Russia from afar might solve the problem. It won't. All that proves is God created humanity and humanity has created a way to destroy itself. But the answer to that is the thing I say repeatedly, whether in a book or in person, we need to let go of the weapons of hate, division, and war, and embrace completely the power of God and prayer. And that was one message I'd hoped the rosaries would carry with them.

To that end, with us carrying what were essentially prayers to the refugees and to the people of Ukraine from the people of Texas and the United States, and with the consecration taking place, I thought it would be nice to have the Pope's blessing. But no one can just call up the Vatican and say, "Hi, can you put Francis on? I need him to do me a quick favor." Fortunately, KOC was able to get through to the archbishop of Częstochowa, the Most Reverend Wacław Tomasz Depo. He agreed to bless our remaining rosaries in a mass set to be broadcast nationwide. Boy, it was no easy journey to get there from Hrebenne. Częstochowa was nearly six hours away, and that's on a regular day when there aren't millions of refugees pouring into the country. So we again decided to drive back to the hotel in Rzeszów, get some rest, and set off in the morning.

After finally getting a good night's sleep, the next day the team and I took off toward Częstochowa. We were all sitting there still somewhat shellshocked, so to speak, marinating on the experience in Hrebenne, when Father Jon says, "Hey, you know what? Let's stop by Kraków, it's on the way." Seriously? This wasn't a vacation. There was real human suffering happening here and I wasn't much in the mood for sightseeing. Nevertheless, we agreed. Okay, let's go. What I did not know in that moment was that Father Jon had no intention of making this a tourist trip. His seemingly casual suggestion to swing by Kraków was in reality yet another divinely inspired manifestation of God's leading.

Father Jon took us over to meet Sister Teresa de la Fuente of the Sisters of Our Lady of Mercy at the Divine Mercy Shrine. It's the basilica where Saint Faustina Kowalska is buried. "You have got to be kidding me!" I thought. My home parish back in Texas is named for Saint Faustina! Then I got to talking with Sister Teresa who told me the Sisters of Our Lady of Mercy make it their mission to take care of trafficked girls from twelve years old to eighteen, which they've been doing since 1891. That was mind-blowing! I had just started Goya Cares to help the victims of child trafficking and here I had a nun, who I'd met by chance, telling me that was her mission too.

What are the odds?!

We all prayed at the shrine but before we left; Sister Teresa brought out a basket filled with folded strips of paper, each with a note, not unlike a fortune cookie. She turns to me and says, "I have a gift for you, please take one." Sister Teresa hands me the basket, I reached in, and pulled out one of the strips of paper. It was a passage from Saint Faustina's diary where she recorded what Jesus had spoken to her that read—*"Entrust everything to Me, do nothing on your own, and you will have great freedom of spirit. No events or circumstances will ever be able to upset you."*

We gave the sisters several bags of rosaries and left knowing the Holy Spirit was undoubtedly presiding over everything. I even looked up once to see the Holy Spirit literally above us—He was there on the ceiling of the basilica!

The team and I were all uplifted knowing God had ordered and anointed this entire excursion. I was so grateful Father Jon had suggested we stop in Kraków—what a wonderful man of God. I didn't have a lot of time to ponder all of that, though, we had to get going to Częstochowa. So, yet again, we stepped back into a van with suitcases full of our remaining rosaries and roared off to see the archbishop. We had a mass to get to!

The team finally made it to town, physically exhausted yet spiritually rejuvenated. We had just enough time to settle in and change before we drove over to the Jasna Gora Monastery where Archbishop Depo would say Holy Mass. Just as Pope Francis had done earlier in the month, the archbishop also called for prayer and world peace.

Jasna Gora is the holiest place in Poland—one of the most Catholic countries in all the world. Just as it happens in Loreto, millions of Catholics from all parts of the world make the pilgrimage to Jasna Gora to pray before the icon of Our Lady of Częstochowa—popularly known as the Black Madonna and according to tradition, painted by Saint Luke. For centuries Catholics have given credit to the icon for countless miracles. To be there in the presence of that miraculous image in this holiest of places overwhelmed not just me, but my team too.

The mass was an incredibly and wonderfully reverent affair. Though it was nationally televised throughout Poland, it remained steadfastly solemn. I went up to the altar with the two rosaries Shannon made and gave to me to bring—one in a yellow bag and one in a blue bag, which represented the colors of Ukraine. Archbishop Depo then blessed them both. But that wasn't the last of the rosaries he'd bless.

We brought many different rosaries to the Holy Mass— rosaries that had been sent from all corners of the world. Some of them were just beautifully handmade, like the one made by a young girl who was autistic. We even received rosaries that once belonged to nuns who had since passed away.

Afterward we were honored to spend time with Archbishop Depo by having lunch with him. It was there at the table that I felt compelled to present him with a gift. I gave him a woven rosary, in blue and white, the same colors as Mother Teresa's iconic sari—yes, it was the rosary Shannon had given me. I knew this was what she would want. Archbishop Depo then reciprocated the gesture by giving me his rosary, which I still have.

Then, after a whirlwind six days, just like that, the trip was over. We drove to Warsaw, caught our flights, and returned home.

To this day I still talk with Nella, the refugee I'd met in Hrebenne. Thankfully, she and her son made it to Canada. If you're wondering, her husband did later escape Ukraine and reunited with his family. I also keep in touch with the Knights of Columbus in Poland, as well as the Sisters of Our Lady of Mercy.

Our entire trip to Poland had been an extraordinarily spiritual experience, and the visit to the Divine Mercy Shrine was the impetus for a second, much more organized trip to Kraków a few months later. We hand-delivered another eighty-five thousand rosaries to the Sisters of Our Lady of Mercy and the Knights of Columbus and met with some of the orphans and trafficked children who'd been helped by the sisters. We were also blessed to have attended a private mass at the Sanctuary of Saint John Paul II.

Some days I sit back and wonder how all of this happened and just how in the world I ended up here. What began as one rosary turned into fifteen thousand which turned into one hundred thousand. There is only one answer.

The Holy Spirit.

One minute I'm living my life as a man who runs a food company and the next thing I know the Holy Spirit puts the word "blessed" on my lips in the Rose Garden and gives me a new job—telling the world it needs to return to God.

This chapter of my life alone could not have happened if not for the Holy Spirit. Only He could bring together a series of events like this one—

- Shannon Haase seeing me on television and sending me one rosary.

- One rosary turning into thousands.

- Me taking a team on a mercy mission to the Ukraine border.

- Former Special Forces soldiers taking rosaries to L'viv.

- My team taking rosaries and hope to the mercy huts.

- Visiting the Divine Mercy Shrine in Kraków where Saint Faustina Kowalska is buried.

- Learning about the work Sister Teresa de la Fuente is doing in Kraków to help trafficked children.

- Visiting Częstochowa and the Jasna Gora Monastery.

- Seeing the icon of Our Lady of Częstochowa.

- Meeting the Archbishop of Częstochowa, the Most Reverend Wacław Depo.

There is no way that this kid born in Teaneck, New Jersey, could do any of this without God. He has a mission for me.

I just listened to His voice and obeyed.

Saving the Children

CHAPTER 10

SOUND OF FREEDOM.

"God's children are not for sale."

—*Tim Ballard*

When I was a child, and I went into great detail earlier about this, I grew up "privileged" in that I had incredibly loving parents. It's almost impossible to describe my childhood living with these two amazing people who showered me and my siblings with unconditional love and who protected us in every possible way. So, that said, it's almost impossible for me to comprehend any child being treated differently than what was my experience. But sadly, that happens for children every minute of every day.

For a child to not receive unconditional love, be abused, be sold, be exploited, be dismembered, be killed, be devalued, be abandoned, be betrayed, be beaten, be starved, and be tortured, is not in my realm of comprehension or understanding.

I have a heart for children; after all, I do have six of my own and fourteen grandchildren. I can't begin to describe the unimaginable joy each one of them brings me. From my grown children, each of whom has made me proud beyond words, to my young grandchildren in whose eyes I see hope, innocence, and a future chock full of possibility, they are precious gifts from God, as all children are. Like most any father or grandfather, I would do absolutely anything to protect each and every one of them. So my heart was utterly devastated and forever changed once I learned about the incredible evil of trafficking, exploitation, greed, and the physical and mental destruction of the precious child—God's gift to humanity!

I couldn't imagine anyone wanting to deliberately hurt an innocent child, but then a chance invitation to a film screening changed all that.

One September night during Donald Trump's second year in office I was invited to a reception at the White House celebrating Hispanic Heritage Month. The celebratory reception for Hispanic Heritage Month is held every year in the East Room, which isn't just the largest state room in the White House but also one of the most truly iconic in terms of history. Abraham Lincoln held many a soiree in that room. John F. Kennedy laid in state there, and the Civil Rights Act of 1964 was signed into law by Lyndon Johnson just a few feet from where I was now standing, which was under the most ornate chandeliers I've ever seen.

There I was among a who's who of political power players when I spotted my old friend Eduardo Verástegui across the room. If you're Hispanic you likely know him as a singer, telenovela actor, film producer, conservative political activist, and independent Mexican presidential candidate. I first met Eduardo around the time he was starring in *Bella*, a pro-life film about two people brought together by an unborn child. In his review of *Bella*, the late Roger Ebert described Eduardo as "the next Antonio Banderas."[4] Early in Eduardo's career, he was known primarily as the good-looking shirtless guy in telenovelas, but a conversation with a tutor teaching him English would change his life's purpose forever. One day this tutor asked, "If you have a daughter, what kind of man would you want her to marry?" Eduardo answered, "Basically, Prince Charming." She then asked him, "Is that you?" He knew it wasn't as he'd been a bit of a lothario for most of his adult life. This conversation prompted Eduardo to think about how he'd treated people, particularly women. Now when he speaks to groups, he talks about the importance of respecting women and apologizes for not having done so early in his career. He also committed to making films that were morally right and decent.

I hadn't seen Eduardo in a while so after we'd finished exchanging pleasantries I asked him what he'd been up to. He began telling me about this film project he was working on about a guy named Tim Ballard who was rescuing children. Admittedly, at the time, I'd never heard of the guy. Eduardo told me horror stories, real-life events, about how children were being kidnapped and exploited and it just chilled me to the bone. Again, I simply couldn't comprehend the notion that anyone would want to exploit a child. But as I'd soon learn, every day someone does just that, and the problem is more widespread than is humanly comprehensible.

Eduardo said the project he was working on was a film he'd produced, in which he also acted, called *Sound of Freedom*.

---

4   Roger Ebert, "Never trust a review written by a pregnant man," *Chicago Sun-Times,* October 25, 2007.

It starred Jim Caviezel as Ballard, who I now knew was the former federal agent who founded Operation Underground Railroad, a group that rescues children from trafficking. *Sound of Freedom* tells the story of Ballard's efforts to rescue a little Honduran girl from her captors and uses it to highlight the bigger picture—the inconvenient and horrifying truth of international child trafficking.

This isn't exactly the topic of conversation I was expecting from a Hispanic Heritage Month event but I'm glad I'd heard about it. After I left the White House and returned to my hotel, I was up most of the night pondering what was happening to those children. Very clearly, they needed help and their stories had to be told. I believed, as I still do, that if more people knew what was happening there'd be an unstoppable movement to end it.

Eduardo and I would catch up again not long after that White House event. When we did, he told me how he was working relentlessly to get *Sound of Freedom* out to the public. It had not been easy. At that time the film had yet to be released and Eduardo had spent about three years knocking on doors but was repeatedly rejected. Initially, 20th Century Fox was going to distribute *Sound of Freedom* across Latin America, but the company was sold to Disney before that could happen. Then, as one would expect from one of the wokest, most tone-deaf companies in the world, Disney buried it.

Eduardo and his partners wanted to be free from Disney so they did everything they could to get someone to help them buy back the rights, but they were getting nowhere. They held several *Sound of Freedom* screenings to try to drum up interest, and Eduardo asked me to attend one. While he couldn't attend the first screening I attended, Jim Caviezel did! I mean this guy played Jesus in *The Passion of the Christ*. I looked over and there was journalist Lara Logan. This was kind of a big deal. My excitement was soon tempered though as the lights went down in the theater.

Once *Sound of Freedom*'s end credits rolled, I couldn't believe what I'd just seen—so powerful, captivating, and heartbreaking. To see what was being done to those innocent children saddened and angered me. I've quoted Mother Teresa for what seems like a million times about the need to bring the children back to the center of our care and concern.

Now that I'd become aware of the crisis of child trafficking and exploitation, I absolutely had to be involved in spreading the word to try to help prevent it. In my mind, that was a clear call from Mother Teresa herself. So I started an initiative with the intention to not just raise awareness of child trafficking but to also offer tangible assistance to those who needed it. It would be called Goya Cares.

I learned the United States is the biggest consumer of sex trafficking in the world, and that Mexico is its biggest provider. California, Texas, Florida, Georgia, and New York have the highest rates of human trafficking in the country, and half of the victims are children.

Not only is the United States the biggest consumer of sex trafficking, but according to Health and Human Services (HHS) whistleblower, Tara Lee Rodas, it is also complicit in it. "Whether intentional or not, it can be argued that the US Government has become the middleman in a large scale, multi-billion-dollar, child trafficking operation run by bad actors seeking to profit off the lives of children," she told The House Judiciary Subcommittee on Immigration Integrity, Security, and Enforcement on April 26, 2023. Her testimony was part of a congressional hearing on the unprecedented surge of unaccompanied alien children at the southwest border and how open-border policies enable the exploitation of those children.

Rodas testified that as part of Operation Artemis, the Biden administration effort to process unaccompanied migrant children, she was deployed to the Fairplex Emergency Intake Site in Pomona, California, and was stunned by what she saw there. "I thought I was going to help place children in loving homes," she said, "Instead, I discovered that children are being trafficked through a sophisticated network that begins with being recruited in home country, smuggled to the US border, and ends when [Office of Refugee Resettlement] delivers a child to a sponsors—some sponsors are criminals and traffickers and members of Transnational Criminal Organizations. Some sponsors view children as commodities and assets to be used for earning income."

Yet, the Biden administration has pushed to get the migrant kids to those sponsors even more quickly and more efficiently. Can you imagine that? The current head of the HHS, Xavier Becerra, wants the processing of the children to run like an assembly line. In a leaked video of an HHS staff meeting reported by the *New York Times*, Becerra said, "If Henry Ford had seen this in his plants, he would have never become famous and rich. This is not the way you do an assembly line. And kids aren't widgets, I get it, but we can do far better than this."[5] Wow. This guy wanted to treat the processing of children like a car assembly line? When Becerra appeared before the House Energy and Commerce Subcommittee on Oversight and Investigations, Congressman Morgan Griffith of Virginia didn't mince his words when telling him that this was "a damning statement." Becerra explained that he wasn't talking about the children but rather the process and its inefficiency.

Still, what's truly unforgivable is, according to another report by the *New York Times*,[6] the White House and federal agencies were repeatedly alerted to signs of children at risk, and that the warnings were ignored or missed. Few things, if any, are worse than the exploitation of a child, especially when the government knows about it and does nothing. When Rodas discovered it firsthand, she couldn't stand idly by and do nothing. "Realizing that we were not offering children the American dream, but instead putting them into modern-day slavery with wicked overlords was a terrible revelation. These children are a captive victim population, with no access to law enforcement or knowledge of their rights. They are extorted, exploited, abused, neglected, and trafficked. This is why I blew the whistle."

Keeping children, and all Americans, safe from those who would do them harm is a difficult task, especially at the

---

5   Hannah Dreier, "Alone and Exploited, Migrant Children Work Brutal Jobs Across the U.S." *New York Times*, February 25, 2023.

6   Hannah Dreier, "As Migrant Children Were Put to Work, U.S. Ignored Warnings," *The New York Times*, April 17, 2023.

southern border. While the Trump administration's efforts made the border the safest in modern history, the situation got worse, much worse, when the Biden administration took over. They opened the border and stopped enforcing federal immigration law.

Biden's administration has become a modern-day version of the Ku Klux Klan that targets Hispanics. Like the KKK, life means nothing to them. It has no value. Hispanic children are being plucked from the border and Biden turns a blind eye as traffickers sell them into slavery. He just doesn't care.

The administration's "do nothing" border policy is, for all intents and purposes, putting Hispanics in chains, and has essentially created a modern-day chain gang of children where hard labor is substituted with indescribable acts of forced perversity.

We have millions of people raiding the border, and don't fool yourself, they're not all freedom seekers. It's not as though all of these people in other countries woke up one morning and said, "Hey, let's go to the United States. Things are tough here." No, human trafficking is a $250 billion business, right up there alongside drug trafficking and arms sales, so at the end of the day, it's about the money. It's always about the money.

Every hour of every day millions of innocent children suffer unspeakable atrocities just so some vile, soulless adults can get rich, and Joe Biden doesn't give a damn.

Sound of Freedom was the spark that ignited Goya Cares. I decided to put together a team from within Goya to begin building it starting with Rafael Toro, our national director of public relations. It also included, among others, Luz Rosario, who oversees our plant in Texas and is one of my closest confidants; Goya's director of public relations for Texas, Mayte Sera Weitzman, who you'll remember facilitated the trip to Ukraine to deliver the rosaries; and Goya's outside public relations consultant, Ally Brito, who in a lot of ways is like my right hand. I explained to each of them what I was thinking, and they immediately got on board. As parents themselves, they were equally as horrified by what was happening to those children and wanted to help in any way they could. We had several people involved in launching Goya Cares, with each of them working relentlessly to get it off the ground. We built a coalition of community organizations and businesses for the singular purpose of showing solidarity for one major cause—the eradication of child trafficking.

Every group in the coalition works hard in spreading the word about the growing epidemic and its dangers, particularly with children, and works to address the mental health challenges that victims must deal with every day. They all also support preventive education. To that end we work with groups like Crimestoppers that go into the schools with full lesson programs and educational videos. Another group in particular we work with that has done an incredible job in that area is the Monique Burr Foundation for Children based in Jacksonville, Florida. They specialize in what they call "evidence-based and evidence-informed prevention education programs" to protect children and teens from becoming victims. They've been a fantastic part of the Goya Cares coalition as have the countless other groups who've selflessly dedicated themselves to helping children.

The horror of the trafficking epidemic truly hit close to home when the daughter of a Goya account manager was drugged, kidnapped, and trafficked at college. Six years later she was murdered. Charles Ezell, and his wife Elsa, then founded Meant to Soar, which devotes itself to creating healing experiences for children impacted by parental drug addiction or trafficking, and as a lasting legacy for their beloved daughter, Britta. They are now an important part of the Goya Cares coalition.

Goya Cares was, and is, a gift provided by God. He gives each of us assignments and if you're an obedient, willing participant, He'll provide everything you'll need to fulfill that assignment. In the case of Goya Cares, I marvel at how what began as a visit to the White House to celebrate Hispanic heritage ultimately turned into a massive effort to rid the world of child trafficking. That sort of thing doesn't happen by accident.

It's not an accident that my seemingly fortuitous meeting with Eduardo happened at an event hosted by President Trump. During his presidency, he did more to tackle the issue of trafficking than any president before or after him. In 2020, he presented his National Action Plan to Combat Human Trafficking that laid out specific action items to end trafficking by concentrating on three priorities—prevention, protection, and prosecution. He gave the Department of Justice the biggest grant package ever to help in the fight, which included the first-ever grants for safe housing for the trafficking survivors who needed it. President Trump also signed several pieces of bipartisan legislation to combat trafficking here in the United

States and in other countries. His daughter, Ivanka, has called human trafficking the "gravest of human rights violations."

The Holy Spirit continues opening doors to bring the message about trafficking to the masses. It's just so incredible that a guy who runs a food company gets calls from television networks, local television stations, news publications, and various community groups to speak about trafficking and the efforts to end it.

I was thinking about that on one cold January morning in 2024 as I walked into The News Building—the 42nd Street headquarters of WPIX-TV in New York City. I'd been invited to appear on the station's morning news program for a segment on Human Trafficking Awareness Month. I did not go alone though. I brought along a wonderful woman named María Trusa who founded the nonprofit group, Yo Digo No Más, which translated means "I Say No More." She is one of the strongest, most extraordinary people I've ever met and is a bright light of hope in a very dark world. María survived being trafficked and her story of survival is as inspirational as it is heartbreaking. María shared how when she was just nine years old her own father sold her four-year-old brother to one of his friends, but she stood in his way and refused to let the man take her brother. So this degenerate took María instead. He plied her with alcohol—a full bottle of whiskey—and repeatedly raped her. As María tells it, "He destroyed my little body." Over the years she's told her story at least five hundred times and it never gets any easier or less emotional, but it remains just as powerful. María is committed to telling her story because, as she says, "It's about protecting the innocence of the children."

A couple of days after our WPIX segment, María shared her story again, this time for a national audience, when she and I were guests on *Fox & Friends Weekend*. No matter how many times I've heard María's story, it still hits me hard. I once again sat there riveted as she told it for the Fox audience, and I could tell it affected host Rachel Campos-Duffy and the studio production crew as well. This is what it's all about—getting those very real stories out there, making an impact, and hoping the impact incites change.

It's just so humbling to know people like María, and I consider it an honor that God gave me the outlet to assist them. María told Rachel how Goya Cares helped elevate the message she's trying to spread, "I have a stronger voice because of what Bob is doing," she said, "I mean, we're here [on Fox News] and you have to break the silence." I was sitting literally two feet away and I could feel the power of María's next words, and I'm sure Rachel did too. "If we don't make this our business, we are destroying the present and the future generation."

There was nary a dry eye in the house.

Though the fight against trafficking typically finds its way into traditional news outlets, I was once even interviewed by Abasto Media, a small publication solely for the food and beverage industry, to talk about it. Imagine that. See, that's what the Goya Cares initiative has done—fostered conversation many people might not have wanted to have. I told Abasto what my primary driver is in this effort—my belief that "every child deserves the opportunity to live in a world where their life is valued, and their freedom is a reality...we have to come together to eradicate this act of evil [trafficking] from our world."

In a lot of ways, it's a downer conversation. I understand that. But every minute of the day, literally every sixty seconds, two children are trafficked. Add that up over an hour, a day, a week, a month, and a year. A lot of children are hurting. Factor in the adult women and men who are also victimized, and trafficking is way worse than you can count. That's a cold, hard reality someone has to talk about. Even within Goya, at the outset there were people on our board of directors who were uncomfortable with the company's involvement in the anti-trafficking movement. That has since mostly changed. I firmly believe that as a mightily blessed enterprise, Goya has a responsibility to give back to our community—in more ways than one. I've cited Luke 12:48 before and I feel strongly that those given and entrusted with much are required to give much back. Inaction is simply not an option.

We connect people. That's really what Goya Cares is about—putting people together who lift up one another, who help one another, and who protect one another. The only way to eliminate evil in this world is with love. That's our mission and it has only just begun.

CHAPTER 11

WE'VE GOT OURSELVES
A BLOCKBUSTER.

"This movie is bigger than ourselves.
It's not just a movie, it's a movement."

—*Eduardo Verástegui*

When I first took my seat at another screening of *Sound of Freedom* I felt a real buzz in the air. A lot of big hitters were in the theater that night—besides Jim Caviezel there were Dr. Ben Carson, J. Antonio Fernandez, who is the president and CEO of Catholic Charities Archdiocese of San Antonio, and Bob Cunningham, the CEO of the International Centre for Missing and Exploited Children. Angel Studios was making a strong push to get support for *Sound of Freedom*. At the time, the film was basically dead. It just plain wasn't going anywhere. My team and I were still hard at work building up Goya Cares but without something like *Sound of Freedom* spurring a nationwide conversation about trafficking, our job was that much more challenging.

By now, Eduardo had partnered with Angel Studios and they still needed to be able to buy back the film rights from Disney so they could release it independently. They'd launched a crowdfunding campaign and were also looking for some high-dollar investors. Eduardo was hoping I could help.

One day I'm at my desk, and I get a call from Eduardo, "Hey, you want to meet Mel Gibson? Come on out to "the 'Bu!" The 'Bu? Yes, that's what the cool kids call Malibu. Of course, I wanted to meet Mel Gibson! Eduardo kills me sometimes. It seems we all know that one person who appears to know everybody, well, that's Eduardo.

He'd arranged a lunch at the home of John Paul DeJoria, the cofounder of Paul Mitchell hair products. DeJoria is a self-made man who started from nothing, much like my grandfather, and like Prudencio Unanue, he's the personification of the American Dream. To meet a man like him would be a real privilege. Who even gets invited to a lunch with someone like that? Certainly not me, at least not on a normal day. So, one minute I'm sitting at my desk looking at a quarterly sales report, and the next, I'm hopping onto a plane bound for Los Angeles and a lunch in Malibu. Yet another of those wondrous opportunities made possible because the Holy Spirit placed the word "blessed" on my lips at the White House.

Everything seemed just so surreal as my plane made its approach into LAX. It didn't matter that I've visited California an endless number of times or that I once briefly lived in Orange County—flying in this time, I found myself staring out the window with a decidedly different perspective and a profound sense of anticipation. As the plane passed over the massive SoFi Stadium with its impressive architectural display of steel and glass, I caught a glimpse of the stunning Pacific coastline and a bird's-eye view of Malibu, where I'd soon be dining with John Paul and Mel.

Once I'd landed, I rented a car and drove over to Eduardo's place on the beach, picked him up, and we hit the road on the Pacific Coast Highway. Once we navigated through a congested mix of locals and lost tourists aimlessly looking for beach parking, we opened it up and were on our way. We had the gorgeous waters of the ocean to our left and the crisp sea air coming through the open windows. For all of its issues, California is second to none when it comes to its coastal beauty.

After about a half an hour, Eduardo and I arrived at the road leading up to John Paul's home. The road had been carved into a gorgeous hillside and, of course, there was a guard gate that you'd expect in an enclave like this. Once Eduardo and I showed our IDs and passed through, we roared up the winding hillside road, and the higher we got, the view of the Pacific and the surrounding hills became even more incredible—like a painting—and I still couldn't believe I was even there. John Paul's place was at the end of a circular driveway but to call it a "house" would be to seriously undersell it. This home was a palatial estate, a compound if you will, with a $20 million view of the ocean—a gorgeous, ornate palace with a Medici foyer, made from imported Italian stone, that can be described as nothing short of spectacular.

John Paul greeted us at the door, and he was a warm, welcoming, and gracious host. He took us inside and not long afterward, Mel Gibson arrived. I'm not too proud to admit that, yes, I was starstruck. But despite his stardom, Mel is a very gracious guy too. Say what you will about him, but Mel is a force of nature and a true Hollywood icon. His success can't be understated or overlooked.

So Mel comes in, and he's talking about stem cell research or some such thing. All I knew was that he involved in *Sound of Freedom* as a consultant and later as an executive producer. After some small talk, Mel, John Paul, Eduardo, and I went to the dining room for lunch. We were chatting about the film when suddenly John Paul disappears. He just gets up from the table and leaves the room. A few minutes go by, then John Paul walks back into the room, goes over to where Mel is seated, and puts a folded piece of paper on the table in front of him. Mel opens it and says, "Wow! I guess I'll have to do the movie now." That folded piece of paper was a check for a million dollars for another film Mel was working on, *The Passion of the Christ: Resurrection-Chapter 1.*

We weren't at John Paul's all that long. Once we left, Eduardo and I drove back to his place, where I dropped him off. I returned the rental car, jumped back on a plane, and flew home to Texas. What a whirlwind—an unforgettable one that was worth every second.

Getting *Sound of Freedom* back from Disney was of paramount importance—this wasn't just a film but a clarion call to help save children. Eduardo had been pitching and getting a lot of empty promises. None of the pie in the sky deals came through. Netflix and Amazon both passed. (Although the film did end up on both Netflix and Amazon Prime *after* it became successful.) So Eduardo did the only thing he could do…he prayed. "I was praying to God for an angel to come and res-

\

cue this film," he would tell Fox News, and he knew God would provide.

Although there had been a crowdfunding campaign, Eduardo still didn't have what was needed to buy *Sound of Freedom* back from Disney.

But one thing is always true—as Eduardo fully believed—God provides.

I'd been deeply touched after seeing *Sound of Freedom*, which as you now know led to Goya Cares. But the Holy Spirit had been very much prodding me to get involved in the movie itself. One morning I'd been mulling making a financial investment when I fully realized, I *did* have to put my money where my mouth was. But I wasn't interested in *making* money—I was interested in helping to share a compelling, lifesaving message. I reasoned an investment in *Sound of Freedom* was for a cause that just couldn't be ignored. Though this would be considered an investment with an expected return, I didn't really care about that. This wasn't about the money—it was about the message, and that message had to get out.

Sound of Freedom was in the dark and then angels brought it into the light—it's apropos the production company is called Angel Studios. It brought the issue of trafficking into the light so we could work toward eradicating it. It also triggered interviews that allowed all of us involved to talk about God.

Now that I'd made the decision to invest in the film, I was excited to tell Eduardo. I was in my office when I called him to give him what I knew he'd consider very good news. He was driving when my call came in. He answered and after a couple of pleasantries I calmy yet assuredly said, "I'm investing in the movie. I'll give you what you need to buy it back from Disney." Eduardo about choked, "Oh my God!" He slammed the brakes on his car, swung onto the shoulder, and literally began thanking and praising God right there on the side of the rode. I could hear him on the other end of the line. "I can't believe it, Bob. I'm shaking," he told me in an emotional, halting voice. Eduardo was near tears.

To understand his emotion, you have to understand how everyone involved in the project felt about it. For them, and for me, *Sound of Freedom* wasn't just a film—every day a thousand producers in Hollywood are trying to get a film distributed—but it was a mission. *Sound of Freedom* was a cause for which each of us was called. We believe in valuing life and saving children. It was so much bigger than all of us.

That's one reason I didn't want any credit personally for the financial contribution. Typically, with a Hollywood film, the ones putting up the money receive a credit as an "executive producer." I asked that Goya be given the credit, but I was told the industry doesn't allow for a company to receive an executive producer credit—it has to be an individual. That's how I ended up listed as an executive producer of a Hollywood film. It was just nuts. Really. I'm the CEO of a food company! What's funnier is that after *Sound of Freedom* came out, I'd often be at a Goya Cares event or television interview and be introduced as the executive producer of *Sound of Freedom* like I was some sort of movie mogul. Okay, I'll admit that on some occasions, I did feel a little like one. I religiously monitored any news mentions of the film and kept a close eye on its box office numbers. As almost all of my friends can attest, I was like a proud dad. There was rarely a day when they wouldn't get a text message from me with a link touting the success of the film and the number of tickets it had sold. And it sold plenty.

In a just a matter of months, *Sound of Freedom* blew up. Huge.

This "little movie that could"—a film rejected by Disney —went on to draw an audience of more than thirty million in over seventeen countries (scoring the number one spot in many of them), which made it a true blockbuster. As this book went to print, *Sound of Freedom* had generated more than $300 million in worldwide revenue, but more importantly, did something on which you can't put a dollar amount—it opened the eyes of the masses to the worldwide epidemic of child trafficking.

God's blessing was all over this film. Initially, Angel Studios and Eduardo had a modest goal—sell two million tickets. But by its second week in theaters in July of 2023, *Sound of Freedom* was the number two film in America, second only to *Mission: Impossible - Dead Reckoning Part One*.

That is the hand of God.

You had people buying tickets at the theaters and you had a massive "pay it forward" campaign where people were buying tickets for other people who might not be able to afford to buy them on their own. It was unbelievable. The groundswell of support for this film was unlike anything I'd ever seen. And that's not to mention the crowdfunding effort that helped finance it in the first place. Angel Studios raised about $6 million through that effort—the average donation being about $500 with a 20 percent return. Essentially, the investor made a hundred bucks on their investment. No one was getting rich, and it didn't matter. None of us were involved in this project for the money. It was the message, and that message was being spread on a scale none of us saw coming.

Admittedly, there was a bit of schadenfreude for a lot of us when we'd heard that inside Disney some executives were insane with rage at the film's success. They knew they'd once owned *Sound of Freedom* and let it go. Here was the breakout blockbuster of the summer and Disney wasn't making a dime from it.

Like they say, "Go woke, go broke."

The bigger *Sound of Freedom* got, the more my phone rang. I was getting calls from television networks, news publications, civic groups, and political organizations asking things like, "Hey, want to do a screening?" "Want to talk about trafficking?" People were trying to capitalize on the success of *Sound of Freedom* and a lot of them were jumping on the anti-trafficking bandwagon. They all seemed interested in the problem, which was a good thing, but only knew about the film and none of our other efforts. They didn't know anything about the good work Goya Cares and others were doing to bring awareness to the trafficking issue. Someone would ask, "So the success of this movie led you to be involved in spreading the word about trafficking?" I'd respond, "Actually, I've been doing this for three or four years. I started an initiative called Goya Cares long before the film was released." Nevertheless, I was grateful people wanted to talk about the issue and that God had, once again, given me a platform. As always, this was the Holy Spirit.

I made that initial investment in *Sound of Freedom* and in Goya Cares and I'm glad I did. It was a risk, to be sure. But I was willing to take it on the chin if I had to—saving the children is just too important. I did make back our investment, but this never was about the money—it was about the message.

I still get calls from people wanting to talk about *Sound of Freedom*. That proves its impact. Though the film wasn't submitted for an Academy Award, I believe it was Oscar-worthy. It's a very good film and so much more. As Eduardo says, "This movie is bigger than ourselves. It's not just a movie, it's a movement."

CHAPTER 12

VALUING LIFE.

"A society will be judged on the basis of how it treats its weakest members; and among the most vulnerable are surely the unborn and the dying."

—*Saint John Paul II*

At the end of the day, *Sound of Freedom* isn't just a film, it's a statement about the value of life and our responsibility to protect the most vulnerable among us. The message comes at a critical time in our history because as we've seen time and again, whether it's through trafficking or abortion, it's painfully clear society no longer places value on life.

I learned the value of life from my father. You'll recall that in 1973 he moved our entire family to Spain after the Supreme Court ruling on Roe v. Wade because he didn't want to live in a country that didn't value life. At that time, I was a teenager and, like my father, I was against abortion, although I didn't spend an inordinate amount of time dwelling on it because it wasn't an issue—not until 1973 when Roe v. Wade opened the floodgates and we saw some four thousand children a day being slaughtered. Here we are more than fifty years later and more than seventy million children have been aborted, so my father, as we all did, certainly had a right to be upset about Roe v. Wade.

In our house, we respected the value of life.

Yes, Dad was a devout Catholic and staunchly pro-life, but to him, this wasn't simply a religious issue—it was an issue of decency and humanity. Regardless of religion, Dad couldn't reason how anyone would be okay with killing an unborn child—how anyone wouldn't place a value on life. If my father were alive today, I can't begin to imagine what he'd be thinking about the state of the country and how profoundly it disrespects life and decency.

The Supreme Court redeemed itself somewhat in 2022 by overturning its horrendous Roe v. Wade decision in the case of Dobbs v. Jackson Women's Health Organization. By doing so, it put the decision to decide the legality of abortion in the hands of the states.

Roe v. Wade wasn't just the worst decision in the history of the Supreme Court, it was just plain bad constitutional law. The only reason it was ever supported is because those who should've known better, such as constitutional scholars, supported abortion. That's it. They put politics above the law. That's why today it's a hill they'll die on as they fight to keep abortion legal in as many states as possible.

It was one thing when abortion rights advocates tried to sell us on the notion that a "mass of cells" isn't an actual child, which, by the way, is patently untrue, and it was another when they mainstreamed the idea that an abortion isn't murder but "reproductive health"—also another lie. Don't fall for it when someone like Vice President Kamala Harris refers to abortion as "reproductive health care." Abortion isn't healthcare and these people have no shame.

The hardcore Left has pushed its wanton lust for abortion well beyond any bounds and no longer tries to hide what it really believes—that it should be legal to kill a child anytime from conception through the time of delivery. They push for abortion on demand with no qualms about terminating the life of a fully formed infant. Marinate on that for a minute. They want the freedom to kill an infant. The abortion rights lobby has, for all intents and purposes, transitioned many doctors from healers to merchants of death. President Joe Biden, a Catholic, has said he believes it should be legal to terminate life during all three trimesters. Yeah, some Catholic.

Nothing says you don't value life more than normalizing the killing of a child.

People often look past the fact that there are actually two victims when a child is aborted—the child *and* the mother. For many women, there is a lifetime of guilt that accompanies their choice. What's particularly sad is that we've become so consumed with self that children are often deemed an inconvenience—that to be a mother is a sacrifice rather than a gift.

Abortion is almost a religion for a lot of its advocates, who also make the issue the focal point of every election. It's a perverse obsession and as they see it, if we don't get on board then we're the problem. But we will never stop valuing life in the womb because if you don't value it there, you won't value it anywhere.

Margaret Sanger, who founded Planned Parenthood, the largest abortion provider in America, was a person who believed abortion was a sort of birth control to be used to "breed a race of human thoroughbreds" by culling the populace. "We must make this country into a garden of children instead of a disorderly back lot overrun with human weeds," she once said. Sanger embraced eugenics which the National Human Genome Research Institute defines as "a discredited belief that selective breeding for certain inherited human traits can improve the 'fitness' of future generations."[7] That sounds an awful lot like Adolf Hitler and his desire to breed a master race. As a Latino, my father saw the injustice of that. He saw the evil of not valuing a person's life just because they might be Black, or Hispanic, or Indian, or Asian, or Italian, or anyone Margaret Sanger deemed a "human weed."

We need to talk about valuing all life, all colors, ethnicities, and genders. My father saw the writings of Margaret Sanger. How could he contribute to Planned Parenthood? How could he allow any of his tax dollars to be used for abortion? He couldn't and he didn't. My father wanted no part of eliminating the Black population or the Hispanic population or the Indian population or the Asian population or the population of any race or ethnicity. He refused to support the taking of even one life. And neither should any of us.

A child lives in the womb for forty weeks, and we should care about protecting that life for all of those forty weeks. We should also care about the average of seventy-six years of life God blesses us with. We should focus on using every second of

---

7   "Eugenics," National Human Genome Research Institute, accessed March 25, 2024, https://www.genome.gov/genetics-glossary/Eugenics

those seventy-six years to love, value, and care for each other. We should value life at all stages.

The thing is, though, when we're discussing the value of life, why stop at abortion? I mean, we're not valuing life at any stage. People are being raped and murdered—children, babies, and adults. Why focus primarily on the womb when we don't value life at any point? Mother Teresa once asked the most logical question of all: "If we can accept that a mother can kill her own child, how can we tell other people not to kill one another?"

Watch the news. The lack of regard for human life is on display daily. There was one day in mid-February 2024 when I was traveling, and as I sat on the plane scrolling through the news on my phone, I came across an article about a grandfather who was murdered while trying to apologize for a minor fender bender in a Walmart parking lot in California. By all accounts, this man was just the sweetest guy—a guy who would do anything for anybody. He was looking for a parking space, and when he thought he saw one he stopped and backed up, but then brushed another car pulling out of *its* space. The guy felt so bad that he immediately jumped from his car to tell the other driver just how sorry he was. But tragically, the other driver was a soulless, violent ingrate with no concept of decency or the value of life. Witnesses told police how when the grandfather went to apologize, the other driver, a thirty-seven-year-old woman, pulled out a gun and shot him in the face, then cowardly sped away. The entire encounter lasted just a minute or so. Who does that? Over a minor scratch on a car? Clearly, if it's that easy to indiscriminately kill someone for no real reason and without thought, we as a society have seriously disengaged from what's morally right when it comes to the value of life. By the way, twelve hours after she sped away, police located and arrested the woman. It's so disappointing and tragic knowing this sort of senseless killing happens every single day.

As I once told Laura Ingraham on Fox News, "We're basically at war—a holy war, a spiritual war. It's good versus evil. It's a war against the people. It's a war against the family. It's a war against life."

But it's gotten tougher to fight this spiritual war because I feel we're fighting it with one arm tied behind our backs. When the Catholic Church considers its two top concerns at the moment to be climate and gender, it's clear something is amiss. Shouldn't the church be the one leading the fight?

This isn't how America should be. Communists live on conflict like this, and they put no value on life. We, as Americans, should want to protect life, and at all levels. The most vulnerable need our help. There are thousands of children coming across this border, being sold and exploited because the value of life has devolved into a dollar amount. It's all about the money. Look at Planned Parenthood. At the time of the Dobbs decision, it had more than two-billion dollars in assets. That's really why Planned Parenthood is pushing for abortion. It's not about "reproductive health care," it's about the money.

It's always about the money.

But abortion pales in comparison to the biggest, most sordid industry in the world—child trafficking—which is a $250 billion business. Millions of children are exploited, abused, or killed every year. Dr. Ben Carson likened it to a modern-day slave trade—the biggest in history. "There are more slaves in the world today than there has ever been in the history of the world when you look at human trafficking," he would say on his podcast, *Common Sense with Dr. Ben Carson.* Ultimately, what things come down to, is that we aren't valuing life nor are we valuing each other. The most extreme ideologies place no value on children or on life in general.

I've heard story after story—testimonies from victims who've shared the traumatic, life-altering horrors they suffered as children. *Sound of Freedom* captured the sense of what's happening, but it can't prepare you for meeting someone who actually lived it. One of those times for me was in 2023, when a group of us from Goya Cares went over to NASA's Johnson Space Center in Houston. We were invited by the She Is Foundation, an organization sponsored by Goya Cares that collaborated a few years ago with the Johnson Space Center to create a pioneering Spanish-speaking program called "She is an Astronaut" or, in español, "She is Astronauta." The program's mission is to help young girls from low-income homes across Latin America become national role models through science, technology, engineering, arts, and mathematics education (STEAM) and to hopefully one day reach NASA.

Not long after arriving at the Space Center, I met a beautiful young lady named Katherine, who everyone knows as Katie. She'd survived being trafficked by her mother from the age of seven until she turned eleven. What a remarkable person. I can't even imagine the pain and emotional anguish of being sold by your own mother. But in spite of what she'd been through, Katie is a bright ray of positivity.

Katie and I got to talking and I was riveted by her story and just so impressed by her courage and strength at such a young age. Katie was only fourteen when we'd met, and she took such a shine to our Goya Cares team that she invited us down to Costa Rica for her quinceañera—her fifteenth birthday party. It was being held at a safe house for trafficking victims called Casa Libertad. How could I say no? I absolutely accepted Katie's invitation.

I knew I wanted to get Katie a birthday gift but didn't know what to get. So I casually chatted her up and asked what her interests were. Katie told me she played the violin, so I went out and bought her one. Luz Rosario and Mayte went with me to the music store, and as they'll attest, I was buying up anything and everything related to the violin. As we were shopping, we met a mom waiting for her son to finish his music lesson. She wondered what we were doing. We told her Katie's story, and right there in the middle of the music store, she began to cry and wanted to buy Katie a gift. We couldn't refuse, and she bought Katie an electronic tuner for the violin. She didn't even know Katie! This selfless mom was moved to tears, filled with compassion, and compelled to buy a gift—a substantial gift! Such an incredible story!

When I got home, I wrote a message on the back of the violin that said, "Katherine, use your talents, your heart, and all your love; to love and build a better world! Happy Quinceañera. We love you! Bob and La Gran Familia Goya." I was so excited to give her that violin. I packed it into its case, then packed that case inside a suitcase, and the team and I jetted off to Cartago, Costa Rica. We arrived at Casa Libertad, and I excitedly looked for Katie. I couldn't wait for her to receive her gift. "Won't she be excited?!" I thought. I found Katie and gave her the violin. Then in her innocence, she confessed that she was no longer pursuing the violin! Too funny! Oh well, as they say, the best laid plans of mice and men often go astray.

Even though it was Katie's birthday, the violin wasn't the only gift we took to the shelter. We brought gifts for everyone, as we often do for these kinds of visits. Of course, the special one was for Katie since it was her quinceañera.

That afternoon, I also met a young woman named, María Fernanda. She was a real rebel who wanted to pimp out the other girls to make money for herself. She tried to leave the shelter and take some of the girls with her. For years the devil tortured María with abuse, pain, and exploitation, but that all changed in a single afternoon!

After Katie's big party, all of us at Casa Libertad loaded onto a bus and went over to the Basílica de Nuestra Señora de los Ángeles or the Church of Our Lady of the Angels. This is one of the most important churches in all of Costa Rica. It was originally built in the early seventeenth century and then renovated after earthquakes decimated the structure. This ornate and beautiful sanctuary is dedicated to the Virgin of Los Angeles, better known as La Negrita, the patron saint of Costa Rica.

Legend has it that on August 2, 1635, a young woman who was collecting firewood found a tiny, carved stone representation of the Virgin Mary holding the baby Jesus. She took it home and put it in a drawer. The next day, she went back and found another carving identical to the one she found the day before. She took this one home, too, to keep it next to the first one. But when she got home, she saw that the first one was gone. But then the next day, it reappeared in the woods where she'd first found it. On the third day she took the statuette to a priest, and the same thing happened to him—he opened the box where he kept it, and the statuette was gone. Then it again mysteriously reappeared in the woods. The young woman retrieved the statuette and took it back to the priest. This time he put it in a tabernacle, but the next day when he opened the tabernacle, the statuette was once again gone! At this point, the priest decided this was a sign from the Virgin Mary and so a temple was built there in her honor.

The pilgrimage of the Virgin of Los Angeles is one of the most important traditions for Costa Rican Catholics. Every August people make that pilgrimage and millions have heard the incredible tale of the miracle that happened there. And here we were at the Church of Our Lady of the Angels with many young ladies in dire need of a miracle—the miracle of healing. There at the church, they were showered with love and the Holy Spirit touched each of them. You could see their countenance change as the hurt and pain melted away. They felt loved and valued, not just by us, but by God Himself. On that day, María's life was changed forever.

No child should ever have to suffer. The vile people who take advantage of children like those at Casa Libertad and elsewhere take very specific steps to traffic them. They almost always begin by taking the child from their home—many times, it's a broken home. They'll be drugged or loaded with alcohol. Then the traffickers isolate the children and strip them of their identity. They're abused. They have no value as people except to the traffickers who value them as wage earners. Those poor kids are alienated. They understandably believe that nobody in the world cares about them.

We care about them.

During their young lives, these children are sold, mistreated, abused, and exploited. They're sold for sex, for slavery, for body parts, and for blood. All too often what happens to children directs the rest of their lives. So, without people who love them, what hope do they have for a positive future? *We* need to be their family. Those of us who've been fortunate enough to have received love must show that we care. The only way to defeat hate and despair is with love.

It's a tough row to hoe. There's so much hatred in society, and it's all mostly coming from one direction. We have a president who is evil. Still, we don't hate him because we're not called to hate. Yet, hatred, every minute of every day of every week, month, and year is aimed at Donald Trump. The vile and the venom spewed his way would knock down just about any average person—to compel them to wonder whether the mission was worth it. Yet, he won't quit. Richard Nixon put it best in his resignation remarks in 1974, "Always remember, others may hate you, but those who hate you don't win unless you hate them, and then you destroy yourself."

Refuse to hate. Value each other. Value life.

We can and will bring America back.

Hispanics Can Save America

CHAPTER 13

THE GREATNESS OF A LOST HISPANIC CULTURE.

"I'm here to tell you that the Western world is in danger. And it is in danger because those who are supposed to have to defend the values of the West are co-opted by a vision of the world that inexorably leads to socialism and thereby to poverty."

—President Javier Milei of Argentina

My grandfather, Don Prudencio Unanue, built Goya on the three principals I've written about at length here— God, family, and work. He passed them down to his children, who then passed them down to theirs (including me), and we in turn passed them down to our children, who are now passing them down to theirs. God, family, and work have been the stalwarts of Hispanic culture for generations and will continue to be for many more.

Prudencio didn't invent those principals, he simply carried out what he'd been taught and how he'd been raised. I think that's why it's incomprehensible so many people in Latin countries embrace the antithesis of God, family, and work, which is socialism.

You see it in places like Venezuela, which, thanks to its abundance of oil, was once one of the most prosperous nations on the planet. Now, due to its embrace of socialist policies and the regime of president Nicolás Maduro, it's a country where people are grateful for a simple loaf of bread. When a government that embraces collectivism says it'll take care of you...run! Socialism has never worked in any country, ever. It has never provided prosperity or freedom. As President Javier Milei of Argentina said in a speech at the World Economic Forum's Annual Meeting in 2024, "Socialism is always and everywhere an impoverishing phenomenon that has failed in all countries where it's been tried out. It's been a failure economically, socially, culturally and it also murdered over 100 million human beings."

The citizenry that thinks a system like that is a panacea for everything ailing them is in for a rude awakening. What's particularly scary is America is heading in that direction. Today's "progressives" are simply socialists by another name pushing us toward an apocalyptic wasteland, where the few rule the many. Despite what America's ruling elite will tell you, they don't want prosperity for everybody, because the less you have the more you'll need them—the more reliant on government you'll be. That's how they stay in power. Socialism is also godless. Strip away our work ethic, strip away our religion, and you're left with a failed, decaying system that helps no one outside of the ruling class.

My family is successful not because of the government or any virtue-signaling politician but because of God, family, and work. We have our priorities straight. No one stood with a handout hoping the government would take care of them. No one stood and complained about successful people who had more than them. No. We embraced God, family, and work and set out to make our own mark in this incredible land of opportunity.

In short, here's how it began.

My grandfather, Prudencio, was born in Spain and raised to live according to those oft-spoken principles—God, family, and work. The Unanues attended Holy Mass, spent time together, and worked hard. The priorities were kept in that order. God first. Family second. Work third.

Prudencio was smart and highly driven. Like most of the Spanish youth of the day, he worked to help the family. But because he was so highly driven, he wanted more than what Spain at the turn of the century could give him. By the time he was a teenager, Prudencio wasn't content to sit around waiting for success to find him. So *he* chased *it* instead. In 1903, when he was just seventeen, Prudencio jumped on a steamship bound for Puerto Rico to look for a job. That was quite a courageous thing for someone who was basically just a kid. At that time, Spain was just a few years removed from ceding the island to the United States after the Spanish-American War, and Puerto Rico was under the control of the United States military.

Change was afoot as the new century began.

In the early 1900s, Puerto Rico wasn't exactly the touristy, tropical paradise we now know it as. It was rugged and dirt poor. Yet, Prudencio, the determined teen, couldn't be dissuaded from charting his own path. Once he'd arrived on the island, he wasted no time. Prudencio went from place to place trying to find work, but most of the people he met could barely provide for themselves, much less some newcomer.

He couldn't find anyone who'd give him a job, but my grandfather never whined about it. Unlike what you often see from people nowadays, he didn't expect the government to provide him with a handout nor did he expect rich people to share the wealth. No, he went out and he created his own opportunity. Prudencio decided to head to the small mountain town of San Lorenzo, which is about an hour south of San Juan. It's tucked away on the eastern side of the island and its economy was driven by sugar cane and livestock. He reasoned that a food distribution business was a good bet. So he started one.

At that time San Lorenzo was sparsely populated, so it was either by divine intervention, fate, or plain serendipity that it was in this outlier of San Juan where Prudencio met the love of his life, the future matriarch of the Unanue dynasty, Carolina Casal de Valdés.

The young couple was strong. Though they didn't live together because they weren't yet married, my grandparents honored God and worked hard to make the tiny food distribution business a success. But regardless of how hard they worked the financial rewards just weren't there. Prudencio and Carolina knew they wanted a future together, so after some time, they had more than a few tough talks about what they needed to do.

Prudencio was determined to make something of himself to be able to provide for Carolina and, one day, a family.

Like so many enterprising immigrants before him, he thought America, New York City to be exact, was the place to do that. To move there would be a huge act of faith and since the couple wasn't married, Prudencio would be going alone. My grandfather marinated on this day and night, and then sat down with Carolina to have a serious conversation about their future and what to do next. They agreed on a plan—Prudencio would leave Puerto Rico to pursue the American Dream and then come back for Carolina once he got everything established. He had little choice. Their little food distribution business in Puerto Rico hadn't been doing all that well since the island's economy had been decimated by hurricanes that destroyed the crops.

So, like so many others before him, Prudencio made his way to New York City. But it wasn't much better there. Puerto Rican immigrants found it hard to land good jobs, and the ones who did ended up in factories, working for peanuts. Prudencio wanted more than that, so he did something unthinkable for a Latin immigrant at the time—he enrolled in the Albany Business College. He attended school and worked. While his contemporaries were toiling away for near slave wages, Prudencio was learning skills that would one day help him build the Goya empire.

By the way, it wasn't just the Puerto Ricans who experienced difficulty in landing good jobs. This happened to the Irish too. My mother, who was Irish, would tell stories about how when the Irish migrated to the United States and went looking for work, they were met with signs that said, "Irish need not apply." Yes, there was discrimination for all colors and ethnicities. As a country we have come a long way since then, yet today's young progressives believe America is still that way—that it's somehow systemically racist and fascist. How quickly we lose the lessons history gives us. And one thing we know from history is that the Hispanics, like my grandfather, helped to build the America we now know.

After my grandfather finished school, he returned to Puerto Rico to marry Carolina. But they wouldn't stay there. The newlyweds decided to make a permanent move to America. Shortly after arriving, Prudencio took a job in New Jersey as a customs broker for Spanish foods, but boy, was he disappointed with that food. Every night he'd come home from a long day at work, settle down for supper, only to sink his fork into dishes that were as bland as they were bountiful. They needed spice!

One night, my grandparents, missing the flavors of home, had a flash of genius—most of New York's Hispanic community, like them, also missed the flavors of home. The couple decided to open up a warehouse on Duane Street in lower Manhattan and fill it with food and spice they'd import from Spain and then sell the products to the bodegas.

None of this happened overnight. My grandfather was now fifty years old, and he and my grandmother had four sons to support: Charlie, Joe, Frank, and my father, Anthony. The idea to import Spanish flavors proved to be a brilliant one. They'd struck a nerve with the Hispanic community, and the business, which was called P. Unanue and then later, Unanue & Sons, took off. The demand for those Latin products was huge. Their little place on Duane Street was busting at the seams, not just with spice, but with oil, olives, sardines, and other Latin food. Then Prudencio, realizing there was more money to be made by cutting out the middleman, had the good sense to start processing and packing his own products.

The business became more successful with each passing year, but in the late 1930s the Spanish Civil War nearly destroyed it. The skirmish broke the supply chain and Prudencio couldn't import anything from Spain. But instead of folding, he adapted. In yet another genius move, my grandfather decided to import Moroccan sardines from a Spanish company named Goya. He liked the name so much that he bought it from the company's owner for a dollar. My grandfather literally bought the name Goya. Think about that. One of the most famous brand names in the history of the food industry was bought for a buck.

My grandfather put the name Goya on every one of his products—for two reasons—one, it was easier to pronounce than Unanue, and two, he liked the association with famed Spanish painter, Francisco Goya. It also was a short name that was, in any language, easy to remember. Prudencio was a genius marketer. He saw the value in the brand, in the name, and in building a such a solid reputation as a brand that a consumer would trust a product in a can that couldn't be seen. This is part of his marketing brilliance where the name is a reputation and it's guaranteed. He came up with Goya's most famous slogan, "¡Si es Goya...tiene que ser bueno!" Which in English translates as, "If it's Goya, it has to be good." If someone saw a canned product with the name Goya on the label, they'd know it was good just by the name and the reputation.

Prudencio started the company's own advertising company (Inter-Americas Advertising) and, as we still do today, advertised constantly in Spanish. For the Spanish community all you have to say is, "¿Si es Goya…?" And people will answer in unison, "¡TIENE QUE SER BUENO!"

Though the company would be called Unanue & Sons until 1961, it was this moment in 1936, when my grandfather bought the name, that Goya, as a brand, was truly born. Interestingly, to this day, so many people believe that Goya is the family name, I often receive correspondence addressed to "Bob Goya."

My grandparent's idea to import Spanish flavors to the US had real staying power, especially with the seemingly endless influx of Hispanics. In the late 1940s after the end of World War II, waves of Puerto Rican immigrants descended upon New York. Some stayed in the city while others fanned out across the state, with many of them taking various jobs in the factories, and all of them were hungry for the authentic flavors of home. As he had when he first started Goya, Prudencio recognized a need he could once again fill. He decided to offer plantains, yucca, and gandules verdes, or green pigeon peas, as part of his product line. My grandfather never, ever stopped making the most of the mass flow of Hispanic immigrants hungry for Latin flavor. He added black beans, guava paste, and coconut to Goya's offerings to capitalize on the growing number of Cubans and Dominicans arriving in the city. What was interesting is how they came for different reasons. There were two distinct motivations—political and economic. The Cubans arrived for largely political reasons and the Dominicans and the Puerto Ricans came for the economic advantages. That was an important part in growing the business—knowing the food needs of all the particular groups arriving in the country.

We have a saying, "As Latinos, we're united by language, we're separated by the bean." So, if you're Cuban, you're going to have a black bean. If you're Puerto Rican, you're not going to want a black bean, you want a pink bean or a red kidney bean. Each group had its own dishes. You have a nomenclature of habichuelas, frijoles, caraotas, alubias, porotos—basically a million different ways. So that distinguishes Latinos, and that's why we've been able to be authentic by not just having the right product, but by having the right nomenclature. While all those groups may have had different reasons for coming to America, whether Cuban, Dominican, or Puerto Rican, they all had one thing in common—when they ate, they wanted *authentic* food from home, and my grandfather provided it.

Meanwhile, the company was growing by leaps and bounds and with a degree of irony, in 1949 Prudencio would open a small processing and packaging factory on William Jones Street in the Rio Piedras neighborhood of San Juan, Puerto Rico. Isn't that something—that the island my grandfather left because of its poor economic climate would become home to a job-providing Goya facility a few years later? This was done as part of what was called Operation Bootstrap, which was an initiative heralded by Puerto Rico's newly elected governor, Luis Muñoz Marín. Like most governors he wanted to attract business, create jobs, and build the economy, and now Goya was going to be a big part of that. The plant would export pigeon peas, pasteles, asopao, tomato sauce, habichuelas guisadas, crab, and other authentic goods to the United States. A couple of years later, Goya began selling its products in Puerto Rico. I can only imagine how my grandfather, a man who'd moved to Puerto Rico as a teenager seeking opportunity, must have felt when he opened that plant.

Prudencio was an exacting businessman and didn't suffer mediocrity lightly. If you worked for Goya, you couldn't get anything past him. He was as sharp as a tack. Every week as salesmen came into the office, he'd ask each of them what products they sold that week, and how many cases they sold. He'd ask the same question every week and he'd remember how much the salesman had sold the prior week. They knew they had to come in with a higher number every week or face the difficult challenge of explaining to my grandfather why they had not done better.

In those early days in the office in Brooklyn, it was all business. My grandfather did not allow personal telephone calls— all calls had to be work-related. One day, he told my uncle Frank, his youngest son, who was not married at the time, and was on the phone, "Paco, get off the phone!" My uncle responded, "Pop, I'm talking to a customer." Once again, my grandfather says, "Paco, get off the phone." Once again, Uncle Frank responded, "Pop, I'm talking to a customer." Yet a third time, my grandfather slaps his hand on the desk, and says, "Paco, get off the phone!" My uncle's response was no different as he said, "Pop, I'm talking to a customer." My grandfather's response, which is now cemented in the annals of Goya lore, was, "Really? Do you call all your customers 'honey'?"

See, you could never, ever get anything past Prudencio.

There was also the time his sons, including my father, had an alarm system installed at the Brooklyn office because of the amount of cash coming into the building. Cash transactions were much more prevalent in those days than they are now. The alarm system was triggered by panic buttons installed under the desk drawers. Back in the day, this was the newest technology. The system was tied directly tied to the police.

After the installation, my grandfather was told that under no circumstances, other than for a robbery, should he push the button because the police would show up in under five minutes. A few days later, employees were stunned as officers barged into the small office, with guns drawn, and demanded everyone get on the ground. Turned out it was a false alarm. My grandfather had pressed the button!

When the police left, my dad and uncles told my grandfather, "Pop, we told you not to push the button because the police would be here in under five minutes!" He answered, "It took them *nine* minutes."

It had been a test! Prudencio expected excellence from everyone, even the local cops.

While Hispanics, obviously, make up the core of Goya's business, beginning in the 1990s and early 2000s we made a deliberate push to reach non-Hispanics. We hired a powerhouse marketing agency to help us do that and miraculously pulled it off in a huge way—and we did it without alienating Goya's core consumers. After that, our mantra became,

"We don't market *to* Latinos, we market *as* Latinos." I'd like to think my grandfather would've been proud of that.

He built an empire from nothing. That's what Prudencio was—a builder. If you'll remember, my mentioning this in the Rose Garden is what caused all the brouhaha back in 2020. I compared my grandfather as a builder to President Trump as a builder. "We are all truly blessed to have a leader like President Trump, who is a builder, and *that's what my grandfather did.* He came to this country to build, to grow, to prosper. And so, we have an incredible builder." Throw in the word "blessed" and, well, you know the rest.

If you look at Goya's growth beginning with my grandfather's first warehouse to where it is today, it's easy to see a parallel with the number of Hispanics who've now settled in America. At last check there are nearly sixty-four million living in the United States, which makes Hispanics the largest ethnic minority group in the country. As Donald Trump told Univision news anchor Enrique Acevedo during the 2024 campaign, "Some of the best businesses are built by Latinos. They're entrepreneurial." He is 100 percent correct about that. But most of those people came to America the right way. The legal way. Nowadays, to quote President Milei, "The Western world is in danger."

Our country is in danger—in danger of losing the work ethic and values upon which it was built. America, with its wide-open southern border and the twisted socialist ideologies pushed by the power elites, has ruined the philosophy of God, family, and work. It's no longer the cornerstone of the culture—at least with many of the immigrants pouring in illegally every day. America has corrupted those people. They come looking for handouts—for welfare money, free college, free cellular phones, free food, and free healthcare. We've told them, "You don't have to work." The Biden administration has created a welfare state.

At his 1961 inauguration, President John F. Kennedy famously said, "Ask not what your country can do for you, ask what you can do for your country." Good luck getting today's entitled generation and a lot of those within the illegal immigrant population to understand that. The John F. Kennedy Presidential Library and Museum says JFK's speech was written to inspire people to see the importance of civic action and public service. I agree. As an American it's not about the handout, it's about contributing, which no one seems to want to do anymore—including many of our own citizens.

Today, the woke mob would call JFK's words, "fascist."

President Milei is right. We're indeed in danger. We've got a generation of Hispanics that hasn't been raised to live according to God, family, and work and it shows. The government gives out entitlements like candy at Halloween, and that doesn't help empower anybody. It's a failing system that leads nowhere.

That's what's really changed from my grandfather's time to today. It's not the values of the people, but rather the country's corruption of those people by telling them they don't have to work. "You can stay in your bunker." People react to their surroundings and the environment. When someone is told, "Hey, you don't have to work," what are they going to say? "No, I'd rather work." Of course not. Contrast that way of thinking with how the country used to be. It's a long way from the culture that built America, the one President Trump spoke of in his 2020 Executive Order on the White House Hispanic Prosperity Initiative, "Generations of Hispanics constituting different backgrounds and cultures have contributed to building a strong and prosperous America. Their collective contributions continue a legacy of inspiration that is a cherished part of the American experience." Back in the day if people were offered a handout they'd be embarrassed to take it and would decline it because of pride. But that pride is gone. Today, they accept the handout.

The rest of America is now seeing the repercussions of that mindset. Handouts haven't worked to build up our country. And they certainly don't come free. What they do is destroy our spirit and our reason for getting out of bed every morning.

Want a system that works for our future? Make it a point to move America closer to God. How? Stop the handouts and get back to the Latin way—God, family, and work.

Ese es el futuro.

CHAPTER 14

LATINOS TURNING THE TIDE.

"Every disaster Joe Biden has created for Hispanic Americans, I will solve."

—*Donald J. Trump, 45th president of the United States of America*

I f one hasn't yet reasoned, given how many times I've mentioned it, I truly believe my obedience in speaking the word "blessed" at the White House in 2020 when the Holy Spirit put it upon my lips is why God unceasingly provides me with opportunities I likely wouldn't have had otherwise. At its core, this book is about blessings. It's about the Holy Spirit. I had no intention of writing this book, at least not initially, but He compelled me to do it. I do believe God gave me a calling and a platform to trumpet the message that He wants us to return to Him. The Holy Spirit is the one opening these doors so I can, hopefully, make a difference for Him and for our great country.

One of those doors was to the America First Policy Institute (AFPI) which is run by Brooke Rollins, the former director of the Domestic Policy Council and the chief strategist in the White House under President Trump. As the CEO of a food manufacturing and distribution company, typically I wouldn't have much engagement with someone like this—someone who has reached the highest levels of our government and who'd made such a profound impact on America and continues to do so. But on an otherwise uneventful morning, Brooke unexpectedly showed up at my office in Texas and asked if I'd be interested in being on the AFPI board. Absolutely, I'd be interested.

She'd later put me in another role for which she thought I was perfect, as the chairman of AFPI's Hispanic Leadership Coalition. The Holy Spirit was in action yet again with another platform provided by God. I'd go out on the road talking to faith leaders about God, values, the policies of AFPI, and, most importantly, the need for the country to move closer to God. AFPI became sort of my evening job.

If you aren't familiar with AFPI, it's a nonprofit, nonpartisan research institute. As touted on its website, AFPI "exists to advance policies that put the American people first. Our guiding principles are liberty, free enterprise, national greatness, American military superiority, foreign-policy engagement in the American interest, and the primacy of American workers, families, and communities in all we do." How could any red-blooded American not support an endeavor such as this?

My role within AFPI is to advance those policies primarily to the Hispanic community, a community that has become more attuned to the truth that leftist policies—policies that put America last—aren't in their best interests and certainly not better than the policies in the countries from which they fled. There's a good reason why the Pew Research Center found that the fastest population growth among Hispanics in the United States is from Venezuela. That makes perfect sense. Would you rather stand in a bread line in a poverty-stricken, socialist hellhole or have a chance to live the American Dream in the land of the free and the home of the brave? The Venezuelans I've met here have all said the same thing, that what they're seeing in the United States is exactly what they saw in Venezuela, and that the criminal element, which arose there amidst the crime and poverty, has all largely come to the United States. The lawbreakers have blended in with the good people coming here seeking freedom.

The Tren de Aragua gang has been terrorizing innocent people and not just in their home country of Venezuela, but across South America. To make matters worse, the FBI fears Tren de Aragua may be teaming up with the famed MS-13 gang to further expand their circle of brutality.[8] They're victimizing men, women, and children and exploiting our nonexistent enforcement of current immigration law. They've unleashed *their* worst of the worst into *our* society, and in fact, the FBI believes Tren de Aragua has now begun terrorizing people in New York City.[9]

It's interesting how this sort of thing happens when weak administrations are in power. With weakness comes vulnerability. Under President Jimmy Carter, Fidel Castro emptied the Cuban jails and allowed the criminals to migrate to America. We're currently seeing the same sort of thing under

---

8   Isabel Vincent, "Deadly alliance brewing between MS-13 and bloodthirsty Venezuelan Tren de Aragua gang behind NYC cellphone robberies, FBI fears," *New York Post*, February 13, 2024.

9   Vincent, "Deadly alliance."

Biden with his weakness empowering Nicolás Maduro to do the same thing Castro did. But with Biden, unlike Carter, it's not so much that he's weak, it's that he and his administration are just plain evil. That's one reason why Tren de Aragua is here—and they're not going back.

Hispanics already here have taken note. Early in 2024, I'd seen a poll conducted by *USA Today* and Suffolk University showing how registered Hispanic voters were abandoning President Joe Biden and shifting their support to Donald Trump. Those voters were turned off by the extremist policies of the progressive Left, the same ones ruining their home countries. As successful as AFPI has been in advancing America First policies among Hispanics, it's clear the extremists overestimated how their so-called "progressive" policies would be received, and severely underestimated the intelligence of the Hispanics hurt by those policies.

After reading the results of that *USA Today*/Suffolk University poll, I issued a statement through AFPI highlighting how Hispanics were now shaping and leading a new conservative majority across America that builds on the values of faith, family, and freedom—not to mention God, family, and work. I mentioned that it had become clear those principles resonated across diverse backgrounds, and the fact that the Hispanic community is increasingly embracing an America First agenda underscored its appeal.

By the time of the 2024 presidential election, the United States will have more than thirty-six million eligible Hispanic voters—the country's largest minority voting bloc. This represents a 153 percent increase since 2000, according to the

Pew Research Center,[10] which means we hold a tremendous amount of power in determining our elected leaders.

Distilled into its purest form, the message is—*Hispanics can decide the election.*

The work ethic of the Hispanic community and the values of God, family, and work, I believe, are the future for our country. In the countries from which most Hispanics in America have come, it's work or perish. There's no middle ground. And those people represent a significant part of the working class. To be clear, these are the people who came to this country legally and for the right reasons. They're the ones bringing that strong ethic to America.

Hispanics helped to build this country and as a community we're a proud people who work hard to provide for ourselves and others. The disastrous Biden border policy has cast a negative shadow on those who've come here to work and to earn money for their families. Many of them may not have come into this country the right, and legal, way but they did come for honorable reasons. Anyone with compassion can certainly understand the motivation. But on the flipside is an underbelly of selfish motivation caused by an administration plotting to destroy America in almost every way.

What's happening at our southern border is an invasion, pure and simple. People from roughly 150 countries have crossed that border illegally in recent years and already 60 percent of them are receiving some sort of government assistance along with health benefits most Americans would love

---

10   Jens Manuel Krogstad et al., "Key facts about Hispanic eligible voters in 2024," Pew Research Center, January 10, 2024.

to have. I recently met a gastroenterologist who told me the illegal immigrants who come to him for treatment have health insurance far greater than anything our government offers its own citizens, and it's free.

Let's be clear though, not everyone crossing the border illegally is a grifter or a criminal or holding out their hands for welfare checks—not at all. But the ones who are have been drawn in by the Biden administration—attracted by promises of entitlements—as Biden imports a new voting bloc since he's lost most of America with his failed policies.

The entitlement mindset is foreign to me. My grandfather built a company on hard work and not a handout. But as a country, we're feeding this. Give credit where it's due— the Biden administration. It has turned the border into a leaky sieve.

The United States is now home to fifty-two million illegal immigrants, according to the World Population Review, which would be the highest number of any country in the world and 15 percent of the entire US population.[11] Although, the Federation for American Immigration Reform puts the number of illegal immigrants much lower at nearly seventeen million,[12] which is still an enormous number of people. If that first number is accurate, the number of people here illegally would be greater than the population of Canada by fourteen

---

11   "Percentage of Illegal Immigrants by Country 2024," World Population Review, https://worldpopulationreview.com/country-rankings/percentage-of-illegal-immigrants-by-country.

12   "How Many Illegal Aliens Are in the United States? 2023 Update," Federation for American Immigration Reform, June 22, 2023, https://www.fairus.org/issue/illegal-immigration/how-many-illegal-aliens-are-united-states-2023-update.

million and equal to the population of Colombia. Consider the enormity of that. The illegal immigrant population of our country would equal the population of the twenty-eighth largest country in the world. Ironically, those people are arriving from Colombia, and also Venezuela, Guatemala, Haiti, Ecuador, Mexico, and just about every other country where crime and poverty is rampant and poor government policies have destroyed any semblance of quality of life.

Regardless of whether it's fifty-two million or seventeen million, by definition, every single person living in America illegally is technically a criminal because they've broken the immigration laws of the United States. But how can you call a parent who crossed the border to work and to feed their family a criminal? However, for every person like that—the ones with pure intent—is a person without pure intent, people like Tren de Aragua, MS-13, sex traffickers, drug traffickers, and terrorists. Biden's porous border has drawn undesirables—people who blend in with the migrants who honor God, family, and work. What's worse is that the Biden administration doesn't care.

Leftist lawmakers and far-left-leaning district attorneys have made violent criminals the lucky beneficiaries of their two-tiered system of justice that allows illegal immigrants to commit whatever crimes they want without consequence. It's a vital component of Joe Biden's "America Last" policy.

It's the only way to explain how, in early 2024, a gang of illegal immigrants could go to Times Square, savagely attack a couple of New York City police officers in broad daylight, be freed without bail, and then use travel vouchers paid for by American taxpayers to buy bus tickets to leave the state. New York County district attorney Alvin Bragg will gladly prosecute Donald Trump on spurious charges related to his business records—something that never should have seen the inside of a courtroom, but he'll allow people who attack police officers to walk away scot-free. By the way, they should have been jailed simply for being in the country illegally, but New York refuses to enforce federal immigration law.

This is what we're up against and why it's so important to get out the vote to bring Hispanics closer to the right—to godly values. Donald Trump told the audience at a 2024 campaign event in Las Vegas that if you voted for him, he'd take care of the problem, "Within moments of my inauguration, we will begin the largest domestic deportation operation in American history. We have no choice."

What the former president wants to do, and will do, is a supremely stark contrast to Biden's approach. Biden wants amnesty for every one of the millions of people who've come here illegally. Naturally, on his first day in office in 2021, Biden announced legislation to provide them with a path to citizenship. His avarice is just so naked. He doesn't even try to hide his motivation anymore. Entrepreneur Elon Musk summed it up quite succinctly in a post on X (formerly Twitter) writing, "Biden's strategy is very simple: 1. Get as many illegals in the country as possible. 2. Legalize them to create a permanent majority—a one-party state. That is why they are encouraging so much illegal immigration. Simple, yet effective."[13]

13   Elon Musk (@elonmusk), X, February 2, 2024, accessed February 2, 2024, https://twitter.com/elonmusk/status/1753590787130994745.

Exactly.

Consider how robust our economy would be if all of these millions of people were driven by God, family, and work. But how do you get that caliber of person when the state of New York is handing out cash to illegal immigrants? Governor Kathy Hochul's administration allows them to get those benefits under the Safety Net Assistance program. While actual American citizens living in New York suffer through an extraordinarily high cost of living and exorbitant taxation, Hochul is handing out money to people living here illegally.

That should anger every hardworking legal immigrant in America.

While many of the people who came across our border illegally came for the handouts, at least initially, it appears a lot of those now coming have been sent here to be exploited by a very organized group of bad actors looking to harm America. Latinos are being targeted and victimized. There is Tren de Aragua, plus sex traffickers and drug traffickers from various other countries who profit from human beings they don't value in the least. They want domination, control, and money. It's evil. And their lust for money and power is insatiable. It reminds me of what Genie says to Aladdin in the 2019 film of the same name, "Do me a favor, do not drink from that cup. I promise you there is not enough money and power on earth for you to be satisfied." These despicable people will never, ever be satisfied.

In communist Cuba, the government begins its effort to control and indoctrinate people when they're just children—elementary school students. It's an "educational program" the government calls Los Pioneros. The program teaches state and government values to kids from first through sixth grade. Trust me, the values of the Cuban government are definitely not God, family, and work.

To get an idea of the vile manner in which these children would be indoctrinated, here's how a typical lesson used to go. The teachers would say to the children, "Close your eyes and pray to God for candy." Then when the kids opened their eyes, there'd be nothing on their desks. No candy. God didn't answer their prayers, they'd be told. But then the teachers would say, "Close your eyes, and pray to Castro for candy." Upon opening their eyes, the kids would then see all of the candy the teachers placed on the desks when their eyes were closed. "See children, you can't count on God to answer your prayers, but El Comandante will answer them."

That's pure evil.

What we're seeing today is a spiritual war with several battles: good versus bad, love versus hate, build versus destroy, and unite versus divide. Instead of relying on God and love, people have been relying on the government based on fear. That's how the power elites get you, by spreading fear. The lust for power drives them to create fear, division, hatred, anarchy, and the tearing down of society, so they can control the masses like sheep. But don't be afraid. Did you know the most repeated phrase in the Bible is, "Do not be afraid." God tells us 365 times in His word to not be afraid—once for every day of the year. So listen! Do not be afraid. We will win this fight. We are seeing a big shift in how Hispanics view what's happening politically in the country. There's an awakening and it will make a difference.

Despite the border surge and the high number of people with their hands out, proud Hispanic Americans have truly begun turning the tide. Over the years, they have proven to be integral to the growth and prosperity of our country. Hispanics take pride in their work and in their new home. They've loved America and studied hard to become citizens. They've fought for freedom. There was the 65th Infantry Regiment of the United States Army, comprised of soldiers from Puerto Rico, that began serving the United States in 1899. So Hispanics aren't just immigrants, they're Americans. We are part of the fabric of this country. Not all of them have their hands out, and their strength is turning the tide of America.

We're seeing it in the numbers and at the polls. They see the inflation, the astronomically high cost of groceries and gasoline, and the dwindling availability of high-quality jobs and recognize those as the hallmarks of failed leftist policies. That's why every major survey done on this subject shows a shifting Hispanic allegiance, from liberal candidates and Joe Biden to conservative candidates and Donald Trump, especially in swing states.

In an interview with Reuters, Ruy Teixeira, a longtime Democratic political analyst said the shift in perception is evident, "All the data we've seen since the 2016 elections suggests there's considerable weakening of Democratic support among Hispanics."[14] He implied Democratic candidates likely hav-

---

14   Tim Reid, "Hispanic support for Trump raises red flag for Biden," Reuters, December 16, 2023.

en't grasped what's important to Hispanics. "They are dancing around the number one issue—high prices. It's not what working-class voters want out of a political party."

It's not just the economy driving Hispanics further from the left, it's also immigration. The mainstream media paints a compelling, albeit factually incorrect, picture that Hispanics don't support a strong border defense policy—the kind trumpeted by Donald Trump. But that's not true. As Teixeira says, "Huge proportions of the Hispanic population, especially working-class Hispanics, are actually pretty disturbed by illegal immigration."[15]

At the end of the day, the Biden administration doesn't espouse the values Republicans do—God, family, and work.

The Hispanics who came here the right way love America and would do anything for it. My father not only worked for the federal government at one time, but he also served in the United States Navy during World War II. He was deployed to the Pacific and was on his way when President Harry S. Truman made the decision to drop the atomic bombs on Hiroshima and Nagasaki. So the war ended before he got to Japan. His brother, my Uncle Joe, was deployed to Germany where he fought in the Battle of the Bulge under General George S. Patton. And my Uncle Tom, my mom's brother, was a United States Marine who fought at Iwo Jima. The Unanues have always loved this great country and have proudly served it, just like the millions of other Hispanics who value and appreciate what America stands for.

---

15   Reid, "Hispanic support."

It's unfortunate the current generation of Americans are so full of self that they have no sense of service. They only know freedom but not the sacrifices required to have it.

We need to get the country back to that mindset, to conservative values, and closer to God—the values of the working class and the values historically ingrained in Hispanic culture—the kind of values that contributed to building America as a godly country. Joe Biden and his administration aren't about the working class, no, they're about government—big government. Their rhetoric is basically, "You don't have to work. We'll take care of everything." That sounds like a real utopia until there's no more to go around. As the late former British prime minister Margaret Thatcher often said, "The problem with socialism is that you eventually run out of other people's money." It's an unsustainable system.

A big reason why it's unsustainable is that fewer and fewer people are working and contributing into the system. We've got people who simply don't want to work who then complain about the "haves" when they "have not." The top 20 percent of all wage earners in America pay 80 percent of the taxes. The Tax Policy Center found that more than 60 percent of Americans pay *no* federal income tax. None. Not a penny. So it's laughable and pathetic when someone who doesn't even pay taxes complains how successful people don't pay "their fair share."

Extreme leftists don't care about making everyone financially equal unless you mean making everyone equally broke. Their motives are always about power and greed.

Collectively, we used to have a strong work ethic. It's not that way anymore. I mean, I started working at ten years old. I worked during every school break, every summer, and every holiday. It didn't kill me. Today's generation complains about working forty hours. Heck, some complain about working eight hours. We are in relatively easy times, yet we are raising parasites—parasites who live off the government and expect the people who actually work to share the wealth. There's a quote, often attributed, albeit incorrectly, to the late Sheikh Rashid bin Saeed Al Maktoum, the former prime minister of the United Arab Emirates and the "father of modern Dubai" with which I agree wholeheartedly, "We need to raise warriors, not parasites." Regardless of who actually said it, this statement could not be truer.

America needs to turn off the incentives to not work. Handouts don't do anyone any good. Remember the old adage, "Give a man a fish, and you feed him for a day. Teach a man to fish, and you feed him for a lifetime." These days, no one wants to fish. Instead, they sit on the couch and expect someone who actually went out and caught a fish to come back and give it to them. There's a line in a 2016 science fiction novel called, *Those Who Remain: A Postapocalyptic Novel*, by G. Michael Hopf that sums up where those people are leading the country, "Hard times create strong men, strong men create good times, good times create weak men, and weak men create hard times." Right now, we have an entire generation of weak people creating hard times.

Our unemployment numbers are nonsense because a huge number of unemployed people aren't even looking for work. Human beings are supposed to have a purpose. Did God really breathe life into us just for us to sit in a room and play video games or lay there expecting a handout?

There is a bigger picture, though, beyond the economics. You also have to consider the morality issues at play. The extreme Left pushes immoral ideologies such as abortion and tries to mainstream them. They turn a blind eye to trafficking. You know who the most targeted group is for trafficking? Hispanics, because they're the most vulnerable. And the United States is the biggest consumer.

What's the solution to any of this?

God. Family. Work.

These cornerstone values that built this nation under God are really the answer, but how do we get society to return to them?

For one, we need a strong leader to carry the torch and lead the way. I believe Donald Trump is that leader. He's about the working class. He values life and family. And he is the man, as the Hermit of Loreto prophesied, who will lead America back to God. The former president covers it all— God, family, and work.

As you know, I first met him because I very much wanted the president to get close to the Hispanic community, mainly the Puerto Rican community, because I'd lived in Puerto Rico for ten years. I moved there in 1980 to work at our facility just south of San Juan proper in a suburb called Bayamón.

My wife and I had been married for couple of years and our daughter had just turned a year old. She and one of my sons were born stateside—but our four other children were all born in Puerto Rico. So you can see why I had an interest in President Trump getting closer to the Puerto Rican community. Though I attended that Hispanic Heritage Month event at the White House in 2017 I didn't get to actually meet the president, not until that infamous day when the Holy Spirit put the word "blessed" upon my lips in the Rose Garden.

My relationship with Donald Trump escalated from there and I can assuredly say that he's not just very much invested in Hispanic prosperity and our values but he also loves us and this great country. We're blessed because, God willing, he will return America to those values and restore our purpose, both as a society and as individuals.

CHAPTER 15

THE HISPANIC RED WAVE?

*"Nothing great is ever achieved with-
out much enduring."*

—*Saint Catherine of Siena*

It was a brisk morning in March of 2024 when I woke up, brewed a cup of Café Goya in my kitchen, and made my way out to the patio to scan the day's headlines before I left for the office. Under a warm Texas sun, I tabbed through various news sites on my tablet when one headline came jumping off the screen trumpeting something that was already known by anyone paying the least bit of attention to our current polit-ical climate, "Latinos, Shifting Toward Trump, Land at the Center of the 2024 Campaign." Yes, Hispanic allegiance to Joe Biden was falling dramatically. The article in the *New York Times* talked about how Donald Trump's growing stand-ing with Hispanics showed him winning about 40 percent of their votes, which was the highest level for any Republican in twenty years.[16] This says a lot about how far Trump's relation-ship with our community has come and the strides he's made since Cinco de Mayo in 2016 when he posed for a photo with

---

16   Jennifer Medina and Ruth Igielnik, "Latinos, Shifting Toward Trump, Land at the Center of the 2024 Campaign," *New York Times.* March 14, 2024.

a taco bowl from the Trump Grill and captioned it, "I Love Hispanics."

I took another sip of my coffee, read the article, and pondered just exactly why Latin allegiance is shifting away from Joe Biden. For one, the Latino community has awakened to the reality that it's being exploited and abused. Look no further than our southern border and the horrifying number of Hispanics being forced into slavery by traffickers as the Biden administration stands idly by and does nothing. As whistleblower Tara Lee Rodas testified, the United States is complicit in this atrocity, which in itself is an atrocity. Furthermore, the administration exploits the Hispanic community by pandering for votes by promising amnesty for millions of undocumented migrants. Make no mistake, Joe Biden doesn't truly care about their real needs—he only cares about whether they cast a ballot with a "D" beside the name. And candidly, I don't know why Hispanics would—I mean, high inflation, an open border, new wars, division, the working class under attack, and life not being valued are what a vote for Joe Biden gets you. Why would anyone willingly choose that? Unlike what we saw during the Trump presidency when Hispanic economic initiatives were created to actually help people, and there was record-low minority unemployment, today many Hispanics feel the Biden administration has abandoned them.

It makes sense why a month after I read that *New York Times* article, while again enjoying my morning coffee, I came across this headline: "Poll: Biden's popularity with Latinos drops as Dems' rises." The article from Axios analyzed the results of an Axios-Ipsos Latino Poll that showed how Hispanics in the

United States "have steadily soured on President Biden while warming to former President Trump."[17]

It isn't difficult to see why this has happened. The Biden administration has attacked the working class with policies that create high inflation, unsafe communities, revolving door crime, and an unfair two-tiered system of justice. As I've said, with America's largest minority voting bloc—thirty-six million eligible voters—Hispanics will determine the outcome of the 2024 election. And that's why Biden panders for Hispanic votes because he sees the same polling data we do that shows how our community is moving away from him and toward Donald Trump.

Hispanics can and will change the course of our country.

The difference between the conservative side of the aisle and Biden's side, at least when it comes to Hispanics, is that Republicans aren't making pie in the sky promises for the sake of buying votes. Hispanics, in large part, feel disenfranchised by the Democrat party and no amount of pandering will fix that. Look at Representative Mayra Flores of Texas's 34th Congressional District. She is the first Mexican-born congresswoman in the history of the United States and her father, who'd been a Democrat for as long as he'd lived in the United States, changed parties and registered as a Republican because, as Representative Flores tells it, he felt the party abandoned Hispanics. They want real solutions not empty promises.

As we head toward what I believe is the most consequential election of our lifetime, I know a growing number of

---

17   Russell Contreras, "Poll: Biden's popularity with Latinos drops as Dems' rises," Axios, April 9, 2024.

Hispanics will awaken to realities of the Democratic failures for our community and that they will, for all intents and purposes, switch sides. As the polling has shown, a lot of them have reconsidered their loyalties. In fact, a survey released by Florida International University (FIU) in the latter part of 2023 and conducted by the Latino Public Opinion Forum showed nearly 20 percent of Hispanic voters have considered changing their political affiliation.[18] More than half of those surveyed said the country is heading in the wrong direction.

Hispanics see the same thing most everyone else in America sees, that the Biden administration has ruined the economy, ruined the immigration situation, and made us less safe—from the borders to our city streets. And Hispanics, most of whom were raised with godly values, don't particularly like Biden's extremist policies or his embrace of woke ideologies. In that Axios-Ipsos Latino Poll, Trump led Biden by eleven points on fighting crime, and by twenty-two points on his handling of the economy.

Hispanics by the millions have escaped oppressive countries in search of opportunities here in the United States. Like most of us, they want prosperity and freedom. The future of this country is in their hands and we have to reach them with the right messaging. As Hispanics, we're hurting. The United States is hurting. We see the war being waged against our country by the Biden administration and the destruction

---

18   Dr. Eduardo Gamarra, "Hispanic Voices: A Comprehensive Annual Survey in the United States," Jack D. Gordon Institute for Public Policy and Adam Smith Center for Economic Freedom, accessed May 7, 2024, https://gordoninstitute.fiu.edu/research/latino-public-opinion-forum/annual-hispanic-public-opinion-survey-2023.pdf.

it's caused—on jobs, finances, the economy, morality, and the American way of life. Think of America as the Francis Scott Key Bridge in Baltimore. It took five years to build and stood for forty-seven years but when a container ship crashed into it on March 26, 2024, it was destroyed in less than a minute. It reminds me of the words of Cuban poet and patriot José Martí, "Mankind is composed of two sorts of men—those who love and create, and those who hate and destroy." What this administration, the Biden administration, has done, and continues to do, is hate and destroy. I saw a meme on social media one day that spelled it out quite simply...

Trump is focused on:

- *Signing better trade deals.*

- *Growing our economy.*

- *Rebuilding the military.*

- *Killing terrorists.*

- *Finishing the wall.*

- *Ending human sex trafficking.*

- *Fighting the opioid crisis.*

- *Preventing voter fraud.*

- *Putting America first.*

The Democrats are focused on:

- *Stopping Trump.*

It doesn't get much clearer than this.

There's a stark contrast between the Biden administration and Donald Trump on many, many things, not the least of which is whether they build or destroy. The Biden administration hasn't really built anything, well, other than the divide in our country, and he certainly hasn't created anything, other than angst about our future. Biden's biggest success has been undoing what Trump built. Just as the Francis Scott Key Bridge collapsed in under a minute, it took Biden just three short years to destroy this country. How easy it is to destroy, to hate, to divide. How hard it is to build, to create, to love and unite!

As the chairman of AFPI's Hispanic Leadership Coalition I've been traveling the country talking to groups, civic leaders, faith leaders, and others about the values upon which I, and most Hispanics stand—God, family, work, and freedom. The people leaving countries like Venezuela and Cuba do it because they lack freedom and prosperity, but then when they arrive in the United States they see that this country now resembles the ones they left!

That has to change.

Let's not be sheep led to slaughter. Let's raise our voices as Hispanics and stand together under the values that define us!

Don't fall for the lies coming from people like Representative Veronica Escobar of Texas's 16th Congressional District in El Paso. She is a Biden-Harris national co-chair and helped launch Latinos con Biden. It is an understatement to say she has no fondness for the truth when it comes to Donald Trump and his regard for the Hispanic community. In a social media post on X announcing Latinos con Biden, Escobar intentionally misrepresented Trump's words and cited "his hateful rhetoric targeting Hispanic communities."[19] Really? Hateful rhetoric targeting Hispanic communities? I'm Hispanic and even I know the only "hateful rhetoric" ever spoken by Donald Trump regarding Hispanics has very specifically targeted MS-13 gang members and the vile criminals who sneak across the border alongside the honest, hardworking people seeking opportunity—the same people Joe Biden allows traffickers to victimize. It's those sorts of deliberate mischaracterizations that help to tear down our great country and create division. Perhaps Representative Escobar should take the energy she uses in trying to destroy Donald Trump and refocus it to actually help Hispanics, maybe by demanding Biden do something to protect the Hispanic victims of trafficking in her own district at the border there in El Paso.

She won't. From trafficking to abortion, people who think like Representative Escobar have no demonstrable interest in the value of life—even Hispanic lives. Their virtue is all smoke and mirrors. Oh, and pandering for votes. None of them stand up to protect Hispanic children. No one challenges the head of the HHS, Xavier Becerra, and calls him out for his inaction and failure at the southern border. His callous indifference reverberates through the halls of power as unaccompanied alien children are treated as mere commodities on an assembly line, their well-being sacrificed for the sake of expediency.

---

19   Veronica Escobar (@vgescobar), X, March 19, 2024, accessed March 19, 2024, https://x.com/vgescobar/status/1770125930284912907.

Where are any of the so-called progressive leaders in stopping any of that?

We cannot remain passive spectators as our children are bought and sold like slaves. For every child ensnared in the web of trafficking, a piece of their innocence is forever lost. We must embrace a comprehensive America First approach to border security, and well, pretty much everything. Hispanics are now seeing that in huge numbers.

Saint Catherine of Siena once said, "Nothing great is ever achieved without much enduring." If that's the case, then incredible things must be coming! For we as a country have endured much over these past four years. We've endured the malevolent forces seeking to corrupt and annihilate all that we hold dear.

But be of good cheer. The tide is turning or, better yet, the wave is coming.

Hispanics will save America.

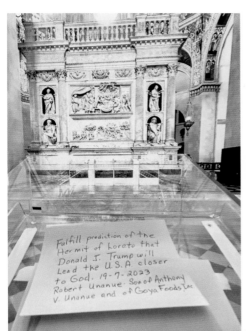

MY HOPE WRITTEN AT THE HOUSE OF LORETO FOR THE MADONNA TO SEE.

Fulfill prediction of the Hermit of Loreto that Donald J. Trump will Lead the U.S.A closer to God. 19-7-2023 Robert Unanue. Son of Anthony V. Unanue and of Goya Foods Inc

LA SANTA CASA DI LORETO.

PRESIDENT TRUMP WOULD LIKE TO INVITE

STUDENTS for TRUMP

THE MAINSTREAM MEDIA OVER FOR DINNER

STUDENTS FOR TRUMP SOCIAL MEDIA POST.

VISTING AN ORPHANAGE IN POLAND WITH MY GOYA CARES TEAM TO PASS OUT ROSARIES.

PRISCILLA ALLYSON BRITO, MYSELF, BRITTANY LOCKE, AND JEREMY LOCKE AT AN O.U.R EVENT HOSTED BY TIM BALLARD.

KATHERINE BALLARD, TIM BALLARD, AND MYSELF.

MYSELF WITH UFC FIGHTER MAYCEE BARBER.

IN OUR GOYA TEXAS KITCHEN.

Liked by **pauljunbear** and **80,649** others

beeple_crap PRESIDENT BEANBOY'S GOYA-MERICA

View all 1,470 comments

22 hours ago

SOCIAL MEDIA POST SURROUNDING THE ATTEMPTED BOYCOTT.

ARTWORK SENT IN DURING THE ATTEMPTED BOYCOTT.

ARTICLE PUBLISHED IN *NEW YORK POST* AND SIGNED BY PRESIDENT TRUMP.

MIRACLE OF THE ROSARIES. ROSARIES START POURING IN TO MY TEXAS OFFICE.

BUY-COTT BEGINS WITH CASEY SULLIVAN OF SINCLAIR BROADCASTING.

PRESIDENT DONALD J. TRUMP, MYSELF, AND MARIO BRAVNICK AT AN AFPI HISPANIC COALITION CONFERENCE.

SOUND OF FREEDOM RECOGNITION.

Robert Unanue, CEO of Goya Foods

THE MOMENT I SAID BLESSED AT THE ROSE GARDEN JULY 9TH 2020.

realdonaldtrump   •••

20,852 likes

View all 1,149 comments

TRUMP AT THE RESOLUTION DESK WITH GOYA PRODUCTS.

Goya 'buy-cott' begins as customers load up on product after Trump backlash

The CEO of Goya Foods sparked backlash when he praised President Trump

By **Evie Fordham** | **FOXBusiness**

Goya president: Call for a boycott shows the division in our country

THE BUY-COTT BEGINS.

HOUSE OF MARY IN LORETO.

WITH SISTER TERESA IN POLAND.

THE DIVINE MERCY IN KRAKOW POLAND.

MYSELF WITH BEN AND CANDY CARSON AT THE CORNERSTONE INSTITUTE.

TIM BALLARD AND MYSELF AT THE PREMIERE OF SOUND OF FREEDOM IN UTAH.

ROBERT UNANUE

July 21, 2020

Dear Mr. President,

I am honored and humbled by your kind words.

Our Country finds itself at a crossroad between good and evil; building and destroying.

I believe that God has chosen You because of your faith, love of Country, courage and leadership to bring our Nation closer to Him.

I pray for you, Mr. President, your family and our great Nation that you will, not only prevail in this endeavor, but believe that history will recognize you as a great leader of the greatest Country on earth.

May God continue to bless you,

Bob Unanue

LETTER TO PRESIDENT TRUMP.

SPEAKING AT CPAC 2021.

Goya Foods CEO: AOC Called For Boycott. Our Sales Jumped, So We Named Her Employee Of The Month | The Daily Wire

ATTEMPTS TO BOYCOTT BACKFIRE.

VISITING SUSAN HASSE IN SAN ANTONIO PICKING UP ROSARIES TO TAKE TO POLAND AND UKRAINE.

IVANKA TRUMP WITH GOYA PRODUCTS.

realdonaldtrump

Liked by **bigmamat201** and **608,035 others**
View all 23,683 comments

PRESIDENT TRUMP
POSTING I LOVE GOYA.

THE REASON I WAS AT THE WHITE HOUSE ON JULY 9TH 2020.

AT THE WHITE HOUSE WITH PRESIDENT TRUMP ON JULY 9TH 2020.

Where We've Been,
Where We Are,
and Where We're Going

CHAPTER 16

REMEMBER WHEN?

"Yesterday is gone. Tomorrow has not yet come. We have only today. Let us begin."

—*Mother Teresa*

Remember when we valued life? Remember when we respected the flag? Remember when we demonstrated respect for the president regardless of party? Remember when a man was a man, and a woman was a woman? Remember when people who immigrated to America studied hard to become legal citizens? Remember when "patriotism" wasn't a dirty word? Remember when journalists exposed corruption and didn't cover for the politicians engaged in it? Remember when we believed in diversity of thought? Remember freedom of speech? Remember when it applied to everyone and not just the people with whom we agree?

These are the sorts of things I think about daily. It's difficult not to. When I wake up, turn on the news, and see the latest absurdity, I wonder what happened. How did we get so far away from sense and sensibilities and the values that made our once godly nation the greatest in the whole of humankind?

Remember when people took pride in earning a paycheck and were embarrassed to accept a handout? Remember when pedophilia wasn't normalized? Remember when children respected their elders? Remember when schools were for education and not indoctrination? Remember when the police were the ones celebrated and the criminals vilified? Remember when we were allowed to make our own medical decisions based on a doctor's advice and not on the orders of an elected official?

Remember when God was valued?

He knew, though, that He'd be forgotten. "For although they knew God, they neither glorified him as God nor gave thanks to him, but their thinking became futile, and their foolish hearts were darkened." The Apostle Paul wrote those words in the book of Romans and it's a fair assessment of today's America.

America will return to God, but things won't change overnight. Evil will still exist, and it will fight even harder to destroy everything right and true. The Far Left will continue to persecute you and to project *their* hatred onto you. It's sad because we're called to love and not to hate. That's what separates us from them in this spiritual war we're in. If you don't agree with their transgender ideology, you'll be accused of being hateful, when in actuality, they hate you. God doesn't call us to hate, He calls us to love. But they don't seem to care about that. If you don't embrace the notion that it's okay for a man to dress as a woman and compete against actual females in sports, then "You're a closed-minded transphobe!" They're nothing if not predictable. For how long have vocal, extreme liberals accused conservatives of waging a war against woman? To support the participation of biological men in female sports is anti-woman. To allow transgendered "women" to compete in the Miss Universe pageant is anti-woman. So who really are the ones waging the war against women?

But we're not called to hate them. We're called to love them. And I pray that one day they'll see the light.

Until then, the persecution certainly won't be limited to gender. If you're a conservative of color, congratulations, you are now the "black face of white supremacy." That's what a group of leftists once called Dr. Ben Carson, and it's one of the most insanely idiotic things I've ever heard. Does that make me the Hispanic face of white supremacy?

If we don't accept and support the immorality of one's behavior, we'll be accused of being "unloving" or "not Christlike." Be assured, while, yes, Jesus Christ was loving, He never accepted or supported immoral behavior. Ever.

Remember when America wasn't polarized? Remember when no American was brazen enough to kneel during the singing of the national anthem? Remember when we appreciated and valued our history—both the good and the bad, knowing that it shaped who we are now?

Many might not agree with our history, but history gives us a better perspective of today. It's the benchmark for how we measure America's evolution as a society. Extremists want to erase our history, to turn us into a dystopia much like the one described in the George Orwell novel *1984*, "'Who controls the past,' ran the Party slogan, 'controls the future: who controls the present controls the past.'" Orwell's commentary on totalitarianism must have appeared unrealistic and absurd when it came out in 1949, so who would have thought it'd be an apt description of America seventy-five years later? "Every record has been destroyed or falsified, every book rewritten, every picture has been repainted, every statue and street building has been renamed, every date has been altered. And the process is continuing day by day and minute by minute. History has stopped. Nothing exists except an endless present in which the Party is always right."

The extreme Left is doing this today!

For example, anything from our history related to race, particularly if it's associated with the Confederacy—from paintings, to statues, to building names, to street names, to sports mascots—throughout the country, has been changed, removed, renamed, or destroyed. We're living *1984*.

Remember when the news media would refer to a riot as a "riot" and not as a "peaceful protest?" Remember when journalists didn't peddle predetermined narratives? The mainstream news media coverage following my Rose Garden comments in 2020 when I said "blessed," was not unexpected. Not surprisingly, the pundits exaggerated what had happened and then used their embellishment to justify tearing me to shreds, and then trying to destroy Goya and our more than four thousand employees. Those jackals did it again just a few months later after I'd appeared at a CPAC gathering in Orlando and again complimented the president. Take it from me, there is literally no story you can believe if it comes from the mainstream news media. Period.

This is especially true if the news is about Donald Trump. A few months after he'd taken office in 2017 he tweeted, "Sorry folks, but if I would have relied on the Fake News of

CNN, NBC, ABC, CBS, washpost [Washington Post] or nytimes [New York Times], I would have had ZERO chance of winning WH [the White House]."

Remember when journalists valued truth? Remember when we didn't vilify one other simply for holding a different opinion? Remember when you weren't hated simply because of who you voted for? Remember when people would talk out their differing opinions without resorting to name-calling? Remember when you'd learn something new from those talks? Remember when there was value in conversation?

The only way to beat any of this is with love and courage. Love your neighbor as yourself. Have the courage to stand up for others who are being wronged—someone else who's being bullied, isolated, or not valued. Love that person. Have the courage to love that person even if they don't have the same beliefs as you, hate you, or treat you bad, actually, *especially* if they don't have the same beliefs as you, hate you, or treat you bad. Jesus tells us what to do in the sixth chapter of the book of Luke, "If you love those who love you, what credit is that to you? Even sinners love those who love them....But love your enemies, do good to them, and lend to them without expecting to get anything back. Then your reward will be great, and you will be children of the Most High, because he is kind to the ungrateful and wicked. Be merciful, just as your Father is merciful."

"Great love can change small things into great ones, and it is only love which lends value to our actions," Saint Faustina wrote in her diary. "And the purer our love becomes, the less there will be within us for the flames of suffering to feed upon, and the suffering will cease to be a suffering for us; it will become a delight!"

And we pray that as we move forward as a nation that we never forget the many who have sacrificed their lives so that we may live in freedom and liberty. This is the purpose that we must have today and every day. In the words of Mother Teresa, "Yesterday is gone. Tomorrow has not yet come. We have only today. Let us begin."

Let us begin!

CHAPTER 17

DIVIDE AND CONQUER.

*"Great love can change small things into great ones,
and it is only love which lends value to our actions."*

—*Saint Maria Faustina Kowalska*

"Ladies and gentlemen, please welcome the owner of Goya Foods, Bob Unanue!" The announcer's words blasted over the PA as an electric crowd rose to its feet in the main meeting hall of the Hilton Anatole in Dallas, Texas. Excited and nervous, I emerged from behind a fourteen-foot-tall video wall projecting the animated logo, "CPAC 2021," and walked across the stage to a podium where Attorney General Ken Paxton of Texas had just finished speaking. This was July 9th, which for me is a day that will live in infamy. Here at CPAC 2021, I was commemorating the one-year anniversary of when I'd made my infamous "blessed" comments in the Rose Garden.

This was the summer gathering of the Conservative Political Action Conference (CPAC) hosted by the American Conservative Union. I'd also spoken at CPAC a few months earlier at its February gathering in Orlando, shortly after Joe Biden was sworn in as president. But at this gathering I began, "Hey patriots, today is the anniversary of the day the 'Cancel God' culture reared its ugly head. A year ago today, I stood in the Rose Garden of the White House to donate two million pounds of food…and having been inspired at that moment by the Holy Spirit, I was moved to say that we were blessed to have a president and leader like Donald J. Trump who, just like my grandfather, was a builder. Immediately, an outraged 'Cancel God' culture had a newfound target." By now, you know the story well. But the message I wanted to convey on this day, which I did in my later remarks, was that our country had been coming apart at the seams—attacked by the woke mob and out of control cancel culture warriors who still want to destroy it from within. "Our democracy has lasted 245 years under God. Yet we are seeing signs of division, moving away from God, and devaluing and destroying life, canceling our history—labeling and hating each other." To see the attendees at CPAC reacting so positively to my comments meant they were likeminded in that assessment, and it gave me hope that maybe something can be done about it.

It wasn't always this way, you know, with a giant chasm between people in the United States. As a country we'd made so many gains in healing the divides of the past, but that all stopped on January 20, 2009—the day Barack Obama was sworn in as the forty-fourth president of the United States. While his election was a fantastic statement about how far we'd come as a country that we now had a president of color, it was also ironic that instead of *unifying* us, he'd be the one who'd use Marxist ideologies to *divide* us by race and by class. For eight years, Obama and his administration worked to foster division.

This entire notion of division, at least in the systemic sense for America, can be traced back to Obama's presidency. As his policies showed, Obama was an ardent believer in the philosophies of Karl Marx, the author of *The Communist Manifesto.* Like Marx, the former president eschewed the "evils" of capitalism, fought for the redistribution of wealth to advance his social agenda, and wanted big government. He sought state control for everything from education to finance, energy to healthcare, and every aspect of the economy and industry. Capitalism be damned, Obama wanted a welfare state. And I must say, he did a good job. Fanning the flames of class warfare pays off when you can convince the populace it's a good thing to voluntarily surrender their rights and their freedom in exchange for a government safety net. You saw that firsthand during the COVID-19 pandemic. Ultimately what Obama really created was division.

He achieved all of that and so much more.

Obama's administration set the tone for where we are now—a country under attack by divisiveness and hatred. It's no longer enough to simply disagree. We must be consumed with hatred for those with whom we disagree.

Once Obama's time in office came to an end, and Donald Trump was elected, that's when the hard Left's gloves really came off. For them, the harmonious days of anti-American leadership were over, the anointed one (Hillary Clinton) lost the election despite the best efforts of a biased mainstream news media lauding her, and now it was time to burn America to the ground—to divide and conquer.

Remember when Clinton said Trump supporters belonged in a "basket of deplorables." Nothing says "unity" quite like insulting half of the country. In that leftist worldview, half of the country is made up of intellectually superior, virtuous, open-minded, and accepting free thinkers while the other half consists of ignorant, redneck deplorables who support Donald Trump.

Imagine being so consumed with hate that you're incapable of having an open mind or the ability to engage in intelligent discourse. Hate blinds people to facts. During the Trump presidency, he created one of the most robust economies in American history—an economy that produced record-low unemployment for minorities, particularly African Americans, Hispanics, Asian Americans, and women. But the veil of hatred renders the other side unable to say, "Hey, well done. I might not like Trump as a person, and I don't agree with all of his policies, but he did great job economically for minorities." They just can't do it. In fact, they call him a racist. To ignore any and every accomplishment made by Donald Trump, or any conservative for that matter, is petulance from the malevolent side of a divided nation—divided by leftist elites in power who are well aware that division, especially by class and race, leads to socialism.

Then you have the media elite, people like former sportscaster Bob Costas, who on the day of the South Carolina primary in 2024 appeared on CNN's *Smerconish* and told host Michael Smerconish that Trump supporters were a "toxic cult." Sounding just like Hillary Clinton, Costas spewed his hateful rhetoric, "You have to be in the throes of some sort of toxic delusion and in a toxic cult to believe that Donald Trump has ever been, in any sense, emotionally, psychologically, intellectually, or ethically fit to be president of the United States." Seventy-four million people voted for Donald Trump in the 2020 presidential election, and if you believe Costas, all of them are members of a toxic cult. That kind of statement isn't just offensive, it's moronic.

Costas, who fancies himself a superior intellectual thinker, as all media elites do, wasn't finished. He went further with his divisive diatribe as he called the former president the "most disgraceful figure in modern presidential history" and "a bubbling cauldron of loathsome traits." Really? Tell me just exactly what's loathsome and disgraceful. The record-setting economy? A booming stock market? Record-low minority unemployment? The historic Middle East peace agreements? Four years with no new wars? Low gasoline prices? Complete energy independence? Affordable groceries? A safe and secure border? Valuing life?

Does Costas consider Bill Clinton's adulterous dalliances with an intern in the Oval Office to be virtuous and not loathsome and disgraceful?

These elites all toe the party line, regardless of how foolish it makes them appear or how disengaged from reality their statements are. It's laughable Costas says Trump isn't psychologically fit to be president of the United States. Just look at the current president. People on both sides of the aisle have observed how Joe Biden regularly displays troubling behavioral traits not unlike those of people suffering from early onset dementia, yet Donald Trump is the one psychologically unfit to be president?

Leftist elitists like Bob Costas don't see that they're the ones in a cult, swearing a blind allegiance to politicos with no record of accomplishment other than making everyday life more challenging for hardworking Americans. As I've said repeatedly, these people are so consumed by hate they're unable to engage in civil discourse with people who have opposing views. In this spiritual war, God has called us to love not to hate. When you hate Donald Trump more than you love America, you're a big part of the problem.

The answer to all of this can be found in the comments I made at a previous CPAC gathering, this one in Orlando in February of 2021, "We must hear and respect all opinions—even those we disagree with. We have the right to disagree, but we cannot hate and demonize each other.... We must unite under God. We must love and build, not hate and destroy. We must come together as a diverse nation of all ethnicities in love and respect." The mandate is simple, they're the words of Jesus from the Gospel of John 13:34, "A new command I give you: Love another. As I have loved you, so you must love one another." Admittedly, since we're human, that's easier said than done, primarily because the extreme Left thrives on chaos, anarchy, and a breakdown of our society through hatred and division.

They achieve that in all manner of ways, not the least of which is the destruction of anyone with differing views. They'll work to destroy individuals and businesses that don't conform. Progressive elites and their Big Tech overlords don't believe in free speech. Every single day they engage in blatant censorship by silencing contrary voices and flagging those voices as "misinformation."

Under the threat of cancelation, we can't talk about the rampant crime in cities like San Francisco, Los Angeles, New York, or Chicago, where gun violence is a deadly epidemic despite some of the strongest gun laws in the country. We can't talk about the invasion at our southern border or the criminals and terrorists who've entered our country. We can't talk about the negative effects of gender transition for children. We can't talk about the scientific studies showing the negative side effects of the COVID-19 vaccines. We can't discuss the psychological ramifications of abortion. We can't question how America can afford to send billions of dollars to Ukraine and dole out multiple millions of dollars to illegal immigrants, even as Americans struggle to pay for groceries. We certainly can't question the documented irregularities[20] in the counting of mail-in ballots in certain states.

Actually, you can talk about all of these things but be warned that if you do it publicly, you'll be censored, kicked off social media, canceled, and branded as conspiracy theorists, racists, transphobes, xenophobes, and right-wing extremists. If you're ever given one, or more, of those labels take it as a badge of honor. It means you've won. The extreme Left never allows facts to dictate their opinions—only emotion. Facts rarely support their positions, and since they can't win an

---

20   "Who Really Won the 2020 Election?" The Heartland Institute, https://heartland. org/who-really-won-the-2020-election/.

argument using facts, they resort to name-calling. Again, they never embrace intelligent discourse—just hate and division.

The ironic part of all of this is how hard leftists brand conservatives as "fascist" yet censor free speech and squash opposing viewpoints, which are hallmarks of…fascism.

This runaway locomotive of aggressive liberalism won't be stopped any time soon. It's relentless. It has torn through unity, and it won't stop until it has attempted to flatten everything good and decent about America and tried to ruin anyone and anything in the way of its agenda.

But here's the thing: though we may simply be shepherds facing giants—SPOILER ALERT—David beats Goliath. I've proven you can stand up to this evil and beat it. These people tried to destroy me and Goya when I used the word "blessed." They've tried to destroy Trump yet he consistently keeps winning.

Stand firm and heed the words of the Apostle Paul, "Love is patient, love is kind. It does not envy, it does not boast, it is not proud." Love others, be unified, trust God, and take comfort in knowing that a new political climate envelopes America, where the once silent "deplorables" are no longer silent. Remember this, the more brazen the enemy gets, the more evident it is that we deplorables are winning the fight.

CHAPTER 18

IT TAKES COURAGE.

"Be strong and courageous. Do not be afraid or terrified because of them, for the Lord your God goes with you; he will never leave you nor forsake you."

—Deuteronomy 31:6

I'd just stepped from the stage behind the video walls in the Regency Room at the Hyatt Regency Orlando when I saw Syddia, Goya's DC-based external affairs consultant, with a phone to her ear and a worried look on her face. It had been about a minute since I'd concluded my remarks before a roomful of patriots at that February gathering of CPAC 2021 and I thought, "Syddia sure looks worried about something." She motioned me over and handed the phone to me, "It's your son." Hmm, I wondered if everything was okay. My son who was calling is the general manager of our Goya facility in Texas, and for all I knew there was an issue there that needed my attention. Though I was parched after giving my speech, and didn't have even a moment to grab a quick bottle of water from the backstage table, I took the phone and said, "Hey, what's up?" He sounded panicked. "Dad, where are you?" he said. "I'm in Orlando," I told him. Then he sounded even more panicked. I've rarely heard my son speak with such a worried tone, "Don't leave the hotel. Don't go outside. Antifa is threatening you. They want to kill you. Dad, you're in danger."

What?

In danger?

He said, "Dad, whatever you said, you're trending number two on Twitter." Of course, my first thought was to ask, "Who's number one?" My son informed me that it was Donald J. Trump. Hey, I'll take second place to Donald Trump six days a week and twice on Sunday.

I knew what this was about—why I had yet again raised the ire of the woke mob—I dared to suggest that Trump had won the 2020 election. CPAC was held about five weeks after Biden's inauguration, and the emotions over the election results were still raw among conservatives. After I was introduced, it took me all of fifty-one seconds to say, "It's just an honor to be here. But my biggest honor today is gonna be that—I think we're gonna be on the same stage, as, in my opinion, the real, the legitimate, and the still-actual president of the United States, Donald J. Trump." That statement, as you'd imagine, was met with thunderous applause by everyone in the room.

Look, I'm not naïve. I knew what was coming. I'd been attacked by the Twitterverse's cowardly keyboard warriors before. With the divine protection of the Holy Spirit, I stood up to them and won. So the next words out of my mouth were, "Sorry, Twitter. I've already been canceled. You can't do it again."

Sure enough, the mob again attacked. They started in with the old, "The Goya CEO is an election denier, blah, blah,

blah." So predictable. Joy Behar, one of the cohosts on ABC's *The View* thought she'd be clever by tweeting, "No more chick peas from Goya for me." As if she's a huge consumer of our products. Besides, it was clear Behar was unaware of the failed Goya boycott just eight months earlier—a boycott that became a "buy-cott" that doubled our sales. These people never learn. As for the threats from Antifa, as I told my son on the phone, "When that dog barks, it doesn't bite." I did go outside of the hotel but never told anyone in my family.

Once again, the animus of leftist elites revealed itself, and it's rooted in hatred and division and the inability to respect diversity of thought and opinion. And once again, the Holy Spirit revealed Himself by protecting me. What's ironic about anyone calling me an "election denier" is that I myself received two ballots in the mail in 2020. I could have voted twice. Unlike some people, I didn't. A few members of my own family also received multiple mail-in ballots. But, sure, let's pretend there were no voting irregularities in the 2020 presidential election. Nevertheless, the fact that I survived another attempt to cancel me is further proof of God's protection. There is simply no way I could have planned this, or that this could have happened without divine intervention. It was, without a doubt, 100 percent, divine intervention.

It also helps when God gives you the courage to stand by your words.

Courage is a curious thing. John Wayne once said, "Courage is being scared to death, but saddling up anyway." I don't completely agree with that. In my case, I was never "scared to death." I was never truly afraid. I wasn't afraid of cancel culture, the woke mob, the alphabet mafia, or even members of my own board who were initially uncomfortable with my statements in the Rose Garden—well, not uncomfortable with the statements but, instead, worried about the effect they might have had on Goya. I wasn't afraid because I knew then, as I know now, that the Holy Spirit has my back. He is what fuels my courage. Fear means you have more faith in your problems than in the promises of God. I'm reminded daily of Jesus's words from that strip of paper Sister Teresa gave to me in Kraków, "Entrust everything to Me, do nothing on your own, and you will have great freedom of spirit. No events or circumstances will ever be able to upset you."

Challenges will always come your way, it's part of life. And if you're someone from the right side of the aisle trying to elicit a change of direction for our country, to stop it from trending left, you'll face people every day who want to silence you at best and destroy you at worst. Where the courage kicks in is standing resolute in your convictions, your mission, and your purpose.

That's what I try to do.

Sometimes it's embarrassing the attention I receive for being "courageous," as though I'm wearing a capital C on my chest and a cape on my back. There are so many courageous patriots much more worthy of the attention than me.

A couple of years after the "blessed" incident, I attended an AFPI banquet, the inaugural Servant Leadership Awards at the Marriott Marquis in Washington, DC. It was a part of the 2022 AFPI Policy Summit, which featured Donald Trump, in his first visit to Washington since leaving office, as the keynote speaker the next day.

I thought that our giving out awards for servant leadership was a great thing to do. Since becoming an AFPI board member, I'd met so many great people who worked hard to further our cause, and I was thrilled we'd be recognizing some of them. What made the night especially exciting was that the people who'd be receiving awards didn't know in advance—it would come as a complete surprise.

AFPI's Chair of the Board, Linda McMahon took the stage and began her remarks, "This is the first time at AFPI that we're giving our Servant Leadership Awards." We were all sitting at the large, round tables typical for a hotel convention hall, and grazing on the standard kind of meal you're almost always served at these things, when Linda said something that just about knocked me from my chair. "Our first award is going to go to Mr. Bob Unanue, who is best known as the CEO of Goya Foods." What?! I was getting an award? Color me as one of those people who had no idea, and, yes, I was completely surprised. Linda outlined a little of what I'd been through, "For previously serving on the White House Commission for Hispanic Prosperity, for his participation in this initiative by the Trump White House, Bob was viciously attacked by the Left and Goya Foods faced calls for a boycott. Despite these attacks, Bob stood firm in his conviction and Goya remains the powerhouse it is today." It took me a few seconds to sort through my thoughts and comprehend what was happening, and after a gentle nudge on the back from someone at my table, I made my way up to the dais.

Truth be told, while, yes, I was humbled to receive such an honor, I was a little embarrassed too. I didn't have any sort of remarks prepared as I had no idea I'd be receiving an award, so I tried to do what I do pretty much every day—speak from the heart. "You know, this really belongs to all of us." Every person in that room courageously stands up for what's right regardless of the cost. They fight a very good fight, and I thought they deserved kudos too. I talked a little about July 9, 2020, when I said we were blessed to have a leader like Donald Trump, and the militant Left's over-the-top, insane reaction. It was as if I'd said, "Let's murder everybody in the country." Of course, to the insane woke mob, murder is not nearly as heinous a crime as using "blessed" and "Donald Trump" in the same sentence.

As I've said from the beginning of this journey, God has given me a platform and I never want to waste an opportunity to share His message. So, since I'd just received an award for courage and now had a platform there at the AFPI banquet, I used it to talk about, what else, courage. "Each of us has to be called to have the courage to follow the Holy Spirit.... We are one nation under God, we have the Holy Spirit, we have the Holy Spirit behind us with the courage to bring this country back closer to God....And this country, we can get back to having a purpose because when we were put in a bunker and we were told by the few, 'Don't worry, stay there, you have no purpose. You have no reason to get up every day,' but we do for God, family, and work. And we've got to bring this country back, and we can do it! Thank you."

I likened us to the disciples who'd been hiding in a bunker after Jesus had been taken away, and how terrified they were.

They, too, had to worry about a corrupt government and a mob of miscreants with no moral principles who were out to destroy them. But the Holy Spirit descended upon the disciples and gave them courage. This small ragtag group of people received the courage to change the world—to change history. And we can too.

I remember one morning in the days following my comments in the Rose Garden, when the storm was at its worst, that I got a call from Syddia telling me President Trump was looking for me so he could talk to me. Wow, that'll wake you up! Evidently I'd missed a call from him earlier that morning when I'd been in a meeting at the plant. I was stunned the president had called but also immensely dejected that I'd been unavailable for this incredibly amazing event. Syddia calmed me down by saying, "Don't worry. They're calling you now." By this point, I was no longer at the plant—I was sitting in my SUV, in my driveway at home, and I'd no sooner hung up with Syddia when my phone rang. It was a blocked number, yet I knew who it was! When I hit "accept" on the phone screen, a voice came to life on the other end that said, "Mr. Unanue? Hold for the president." Wow! That'll get your attention. I waited a moment and then I heard the familiar voice of Donald Trump. After a few pleasantries, and some talk about how the pandemic had ruined the economy and how Joe Biden couldn't put two coherent sentences together, he complimented me for standing my ground in the face of cancel culture. "You have courage," the president told me. Before we hung up I made sure to tell him, "Mr. President, we need you. I love you, and our country loves you."

I later received a similar call from Dr. Ben Carson, who was there that infamous day in the Rose Garden. Much like President Trump had done, he, too, told me that I had courage and invited me to join the board of his American Cornerstone Institute (ACI). I'd later be invited to the Trump National Golf Club Bedminster for the 2022 ACI Founders Dinner where President Trump was presented with the Founders Award. Before dinner I was privileged to have joined the president and Dr. Carson in a private roundtable discussion.

I'll tell you, if you want to see courage on display daily, look no further than Donald Trump. For that man to even emerge from the front door of his home takes courage. Courage is how you carry on when evil people threaten you, falsely accuse you of crimes, work to put you into prison, lie about you, slander your family, and shower you with a constant barrage of hate. To withstand that—staying the course despite it all, because you love America, now *that's* courage.

Just a year after President Trump received the 2022 ACI Founders Award, I received the same honor. I couldn't believe it. ACI presented me with the 2023 Founders Award at its annual dinner, this one in Mount Vernon, Virginia—the home of our great first president, George Washington. What a privilege. Truly. The dinner took place on a cool fall night in late October and to be sitting in the shadow of the home of our first president, with all of its grandeur, and receiving an award that a year earlier had been given to our forty-fifth president, well, words can't adequately capture how humbled I was or how deeply patriotic I felt.

The dinner was held in one of those high peak pole tents you often see at large social events like this, ones that look more like an actual building than a tent. After his introductory remarks, Dr. Carson began speaking on courage and how it seemed to be sorely lacking in America. "When I was running for president I was very impressed as I went across this country to the smallest little hamlets and the largest cities. I discovered that most Americans have common sense but what they lack is courage. People will sit and look at their feet, they won't say anything because they're afraid somebody might call them a nasty name or try to cancel them. What we need are courageous individuals."

Courage built this country. It was courage that drove the colonists to stand up to King George III of Great Britain and say, "Enough!" It was courage that led them to take up arms and fight the most powerful army in the world for independence. Even the simple act of mailing a letter, the Declaration of Independence, took an extraordinary amount of courage. Can you imagine the high degree of stress for Thomas Jefferson, John Hancock, and the rest of the Founding Fathers as they waited to hear how *that* was received?

Courage.

I thought about that as Dr. Carson so eloquently spoke about courage there outside the home of George Washington—a man whose courage drove him to fight for the freedom that came to define our great country. I didn't feel my standing up to cancel culture was quite the same as fighting the redcoats, but still, I was grateful to be recognized. And yes, given the woke mob's insatiable lust for destruction, for any patriotic American, it *does* take courage to stand up to it.

"This individual, Bob Unanue, is the CEO of Goya Foods," Dr. Carson continued. "I first met him at the White House, and he had the audacity to say something good about President Trump, and they tried to cancel him." You know, I think it says a lot about where America is now that the mere expression of respect for the president and standing up for that is considered an act of courage, but that's our reality. "In addition to that, Bob was one of the main forces behind the very successful movie *The Sound of Freedom* and he has been a tireless warrior fighting against human trafficking and a combination of courage, tenacity, and morality is what makes him the recipient of this award. Bob, please come up."

After being introduced, the group applauded, I strode to the stage, and when I got there I gave Dr. Carson a huge hug. We've become dear friends and I'm so grateful to be able to call this wonderful, God-loving man my brother in Christ.

I looked out from the stage and saw some real political heavyweights in the room. I mean, my goodness, there was Newt Gingrich, the Speaker of the House in the late 1990s, and in my mind, the greatest Speaker of the House. For a second, I thought, "How did I get here? Who cares what I have to say?" Remember, I run a food company. But as I've said time and time and time again, when you're obedient to the Holy Spirit and you allow God to dictate your purpose, He will take you places you never could go on your own.

I stepped to the microphone and said, "July 9th, 2020, I'm at the White House in the Rose Garden. Dr. Carson is in attendance. I was talking and I stopped myself and the Holy Spirit put one word on my lips, and I said, 'At the same time we're *blessed* to have a president like President Trump'...I had no idea that this would erupt into such a big thing but when you're called you have to answer."

You do have to answer, and you have a choice to accept the calling or to reject the calling. And it often takes courage to accept—to do the things God wants us to do. President Trump told me I have courage. Dr. Carson told me I have courage. Brooke Rollins told me I have courage. They've presented me awards for it. But the truth is, I don't feel courageous. I'm embarrassed by all of this, because basically, it's not me, it's the Holy Spirit. The Holy Spirit protected both me and Goya when we were under fire. Courage is the Holy Spirit. I'm just a guy who loves his country and is passionate that America has a desperate need of returning to God.

I find it interesting how people think it took courage to say, "Hell no, I won't apologize," when I was staring down the barrel of cancel culture. Why would I apologize for having an opinion? Or for standing with the president? Or for my beliefs? Never, ever capitulate to those who want to destroy you. Saying "I'm sorry," never placates them, in fact, it makes it worse by emboldening them. Stand strong and be courageous. The silent majority cannot remain silent. It's going to take courage, from each of us, to save our incredible country from the evil that seeks to devour it. But if history has shown us anything, it's that true patriots always rise to the challenge.

After all, as our anthem reminds us, America is the home of the brave.

CHAPTER 19

SETTING THE STAGE FOR A SPIRITUAL RESURGENCE.

"God saw how corrupt the earth had become, for all the people on earth had corrupted their ways."

—*Genesis 6:12*

I felt the warmth of the Holy Spirit wash over me as I stood with my team inside the Holy House of Loreto in Italy. As you now know, that was an extraordinary trip, and the Holy Spirit touched each of us so profoundly that when we left there, we all felt a stronger and deeper connection with our Heavenly father.

There's a certain peace that comes when receiving the touch of the Holy Spirit in a reverent place like Loreto. I'm certainly not the first of the faithful to experience it, and I certainly won't be the last. I would suspect that most of those who make the pilgrimage don't consider the journey a touristy day trip to see an old building. No. You feel there's a greater purpose, driven by a spiritual yearning, to understand something greater than yourself. Of course, as a devout Catholic, the aura of the basilica sent me to a contemplative place as I beheld the storied home of the Virgin Mary with my own eyes.

Admittedly, as I stood there praying beneath the ornate marble structure above her home, there were moments when I wondered whether this was the spot where Tom Zimmer, the famed Hermit of Loreto, prayed and where it is said he uttered these prophetic words, "The man who, in the future, is going to lead America back to God is Donald J. Trump." That prophecy, which Zimmer reportedly made in the 1980s, is an extraordinary thing to consider. In fact, that's exactly what I did for most of the time we spent in the van on the drive to Loreto and at the basilica.

Will the prophecy actually come to pass? I believe so. I not only believe Donald Trump will lead America back to God, with God being the only one who knows exactly how he'll do it, but I also believe that in 2024, Donald Trump will, once again, be elected president of the United States.

Thanks to the relentless efforts of the so-called "progressives," our country has degenerated into a place split between love and hate. There are those who would say that in regard to Trump, "Oh, you either love him or you hate him." Well, you know what? Hate is not an option. You can disagree, you can dislike, but hate is not an option. We're engaged in a series of spiritual wars where it's love versus hate, good versus evil, build versus destroy, and unite versus divide. At the end of the day, those are the important choices. Which one will you make?

We see what's happening spiritually in our country. Much of America has forsaken God and has lived up to what the Apostle Paul so eloquently described in the book of Romans, "They exchanged the truth about God for a lie and worshipped and served created things rather than the Creator—

who is forever praised." America embraces the "selfie culture," whereas people serve themselves and fame and money and prestige—not God. Not others. "They have become filled with every kind of wickedness, evil, greed and depravity. They are full of envy, murder, strife, deceit and malice. They are gossips, slanderers, God-haters, insolent, arrogant and boastful; they invent ways of doing evil; they disobey their parents; they have no understanding, no fidelity, no love, no mercy." Does that sound familiar? Paul is describing much of today's American society to a T.

We've stopped valuing life. The country has fallen from its spiritual foundation and God is watching.

Our society should be about loving and building—about moving closer to God. The thing about that prophecy saying Trump will lead the country closer to God, is that regardless of whether you believe it, there's no debate that America has been moving *away* from God in so many ways. We're attacking children and we're attacking the family. All of this stuff about gender and sexual identity—it's about destroying the family. Once you mutilate a female child, and later she becomes an adult, she can't bear children. Once you mutilate a boy, when he grows into an adult, he cannot procreate. There's a war against the family.

Every June the rainbow flag is ubiquitous in American society because companies fear cancelation if they don't acknowledge the pride the flag represents for the LGBTQ+ community. Things meant for good have been twisted to mean something else.

Most people these days either don't know or have forgotten what a rainbow truly represents. It represents God's mercy on man. After the great flood, God made a promise—a covenant, if you will—to Noah that He'd never again flood the Earth. In Genesis 9 He says, "I have set my *rainbow* in the clouds, and it will be the sign of the covenant between me and the earth. Whenever I bring clouds over the earth and the *rainbow* appears in the clouds, I will remember my covenant between me and you and all living creatures of every kind. Never again will the waters become a flood to destroy all life." Yet now the rainbow represents the pride of the LGBTQ+ community? Something so wonderful and holy, like God's mercy, has been twisted into something else entirely. And for anyone unaware of God's character—He values humility not pride.

In America, we've run out of letters and flags. We're so focused on self that we've essentially moved away from God to worship ourselves as we would the Creator.

There's a war against the family. Extreme liberalism thinks pedophilia is okay. Trafficking is okay. Abortion is okay. To them, life has no value. God created humanity and humanity creates ways to destroy itself. The Apostle Paul called it, "For although they knew God, they neither glorified him as God nor gave thanks to him, but their thinking became futile, and their foolish hearts were darkened."

We're moving further away from God. Even the church itself has gravitated away from Him and more toward woke social justice issues. Pope Francis has taken the Catholic Church into a "new direction" which attacks the sanctity of family and life as he embraces social justice at the expense of holiness.

You don't have to be a believer to know that for centuries the Roman Catholic Church has been a beacon for millions of people leading its faithful toward a path of righteousness and repentance. This is a church that reveres its leader as the embodiment of holiness. However, Pope Francis's most recent actions reveal a desire to move the church closer to man than to God. This is not the sort of thing you expect from the leader of the church.

A "rubber stamped" Synod on Synodality, which many Catholics know is used by leadership to make changes to the church and its doctrines with as little fanfare as possible, revealed Pope Francis's true intentions. He wants more voices determining the church's future. (There should be just *one* voice—God's.) Under the guise of "inclusion," the pontiff has pushed a not-so-secret agenda to create a new doctrine that moves the church away from the traditional family, away from valuing life, and away from God. To know how truly serious he is about this, Pope Francis removed Bishop Joseph Strickland from his position at the Diocese of Tyler, Texas. The bishop was an incredibly vocal opponent of the church's new direction, which he felt was part of a "godless agenda."

Bishop Strickland had good reason to be concerned. In late 2023, the Vatican announced that it was allowing priests to bless what the church calls "unnatural unions," which is a 180-degree flip from its position just two years earlier when it defined any form of blessing those unions as "illicit." I submit that *all* people are created by God and worthy of His love, but the issue here is the Pope's bended knee approach to social issues where he bows to the minority and fosters divisiveness by favoring one group over another.

There's a divide within the faith—and the Pope has taken to picking and choosing who receives his blessings from a woke-approved list of the so-called "marginalized" groups. By choosing who to bless, Pope Francis has created a hierarchy of value dependent on which group a person falls in—one group of people is more blessed or important or valued than the other. I'm sorry but *every* person is a gift from God. We are all blessed, and every life is valuable. The whole thing reeks of George Orwell's *Animal Farm*, "All animals are equal, but some animals are more equal than others."

The leader of church should be leading to people to God but instead, through his policies, the Pontiff is leading us *away* from God toward the conformity of man. He's essentially saying it's okay to hate people in certain groups—those outside the ones he's "blessed." Pope Francis, by his example, is picking and choosing who to bless and who to hate.

He's become part of the problem.

As fallible human beings, we tend to elevate and bless people with whom we agree. When "blessed" is spoken by or about people with whom we disagree, however, that becomes a problem. Consider what happened to me back at the Rose Garden in 2020. I was attacked viciously for using the word "blessed."

That's division caused by a hierarchy of human value.

The Pope's credibility is also seriously put into question when he calls President Biden a "good Catholic" and rolls out the Vatican red carpet for him even though Biden has a history of supporting the right to terminate life. Conversely, when President Trump visited the Vatican he was coldly received. Of course, Trump has a history of valuing life.

The church has survived scandals bought on by the abhorrent behavior of the pedophiles within its walls—scandals which continue to plague the church. Yet Pope Francis, rather than use that as an impetus to return the church to its roots, is instead employing Catholics to engage a new theology—a new direction that doesn't necessarily need to correspond to the Christian face of God.

Much of the church's leadership globally doesn't agree with the Pope's new progressive agenda. It wasn't just Bishop Strickland. Cardinal Gerhard Müller, who served under Pope Benedict as his doctrinal chief told Reuters that Benedict never would have approved of Francis's edict to bless people in same-sex relationships.

In 2023, Pope Francis called upon the church to adapt its theology to the changing times, to "the conditions in which men and women live daily in different geographical, social, and cultural environments." It's what some have called the church's "new direction." What the Pope is saying is that because people are changing, the church should change with it—to conform itself to the people. This is decidedly anti-Catholic. It should be the other way around. God's righteousness doesn't change. The foundations of faith don't change. Christ's death and resurrection didn't change. And God's standard for what constitutes righteous behavior hasn't changed. We as representatives of the church are now supposed to say, "Your behavior might be sinful, but the times have changed, so we're good?" I don't agree. God's truth never changes regardless of what man does.

That same year, Pope Francis sent a message to the United Nations Climate Change Conference calling climate change a "global social issue" and urged delegates to address it. He talked about toxic emissions and greenhouse gases and their effect on the environment. Is the Pope now an environmental scientist and activist? Yes, we should want to protect our beautiful planet and the environment in which we live, but let's address protecting life and the family and leading people to God. The Pope and the cabinet he is forming around him are focused, not on life and the family, but on the hallmarks of the liberal "progressive" agenda—gender and climate.

As it appears to me, the church, much like America, is heading away from God. Ironically, even though Donald Trump isn't a church leader, when it came to spiritual matters while he was president, he was more on point than what we're seeing from some of the church leadership these days. He did things that didn't get much attention in the mainstream media (no surprise) that showed his belief in the power of prayer, not just to guide him, but America as well. The former president also surrounds himself with godly, spiritual people. There was a day back in 2019 when Trump invited forty worship leaders into the Oval Office to lay hands on him and pray. One of the people who was there, Sean Feucht, the former worship leader of Bethel Church, the megachurch in Redding, California, recounted how the group went over to the president at the Resolute desk and prayed that "God's presence would invade that place and that His glory would be felt." Pastor Mario

Bramnick of New Wine Ministries in Florida, who is also the head of the Latino Coalition for Israel, told me, "God has his hands on Donald J. Trump, and he isn't letting go."

Pastor Bramnick was also there at a restaurant in the Little Havana neighborhood of Miami, Florida, in June 2023, when Trump allowed Bramnick and other religious leaders—both Christian and Jewish—to take turns praying over him. The former president is keenly aware of the poor spiritual state of our country and where it needs to be, and he relishes the idea of fixing it. He is extraordinarily spiritual—which is more than a dishonest mainstream media would have you believe. He also sees what I see—that America must return to its godly foundation. As a country, we have allowed God to be removed from almost every facet of life and we've reaped the consequences, from rising crime, hatred, and division to the worship of self.

The Pope's woke ideology is one glaring example of why we need a strong leader who will return America to God. Holiness is absolute. It is also healing and unifying. Now, more than ever, we must love our neighbor as we love ourselves.

Because the moral and spiritual fabric of America, and the world, are being torn to shreds, we need a president who values life and who will work to keep the values of our country strong. Jesus Christ wasn't wishy washy. He stood firm on His message. That's the kind of leader America needs, one who doesn't wither in the face of evil.

Make no mistake, progressive extremists won't stop hammering at social, political, and spiritual issues. They won't refrain from keeping us separated by class and race. They won't

stop fueling division and hate, and they won't stop their blatant disregard for life, decency, and morality. Those extremists
desire the removal of God from every part of society and the
total annihilation of free speech. They want a nation that is
hostile to liberty, freedom, and faith.

America's enemies, which is what these progressives are,
want to remove God from the schools so they can push their
own religion—the government and its approved offshoots,
Antifa, Black Lives Matter, and the rest of the alphabet mafia.

But a spiritual resurgence is coming.

While Pope Francis seems content to spend his time
focusing on selfish individualism rather than holiness and salvation, there is an unshakable leader waiting in the wings who
will rise up to take the reins and lead America back to God.

I'm excited because I know just who that is.

CHAPTER 20

THE RETURN OF DJT
AKA
TAKING BACK OUR COUNTRY.

*"Restore us to yourself, Lord, that we may
return; renew our days as of old."*

— *Lamentations 5:21*

During his speech at the 2022 AFPI Policy Summit, Donald Trump distilled the state of America—the animus, the division, the efforts to destroy conservatism and the free exchange of ideas, and the efforts to destroy him—into one brilliantly poignant sentence: "Never forget everything this corrupt establishment is doing to me is all about reserving their power and control over the American people, they want to damage you in any form, but they really want to damage me so I can no longer go back to work for you."

Bullseye.

He's right. Everything we've seen during the entirety of the Biden presidency is rooted in one thing—maintaining control over you. The few controlling the many—one of the tenets of communism.

A Trump resurgence and ultimately another Trump presidency scares the hell out of the so-called progressive left because unlike them, he wants *you* to have the power—the people. That's counter to what Biden and his followers want. See, they want to be the gatekeepers of information, to limit your ability to make your own informed decisions, and to be able to control you. The COVID-19 pandemic was their test run, and sadly, Americans made it all too easy. The power elites limited the free flow of information and censored those who disagreed with the narrative and were ultimately able instill fear so effectively that Americans willingly surrendered their freedom.

Fear opened the door for the few to control the many.

Of course, using the pandemic to gain power and control over the masses was just a byproduct of the liberal elite's real goal: destroying the Trump presidency.

I remember how it began, at least for me. I'd been on a flight back from Spain after visiting the Goya España offices in Seville—and I was tired. As the plane took off, I'd hoped there'd be no real distractions for the next nine hours, although, there's always that one guy who starts snoring before the flight attendants pull the first stowed drink cart from its latches.

I'd thrown my carry-on bag into the overhead compartment and settled in. My seat might as well have been a memory foam mattress, given how tired I was, although the leather headrest was decidedly not made from the Corinthian leather Ricardo Montalbán so eloquently described in his old Chrysler commercials as "rich in quality, rare, and luxurious."

Before I closed my eyes, I looked around the cabin and thought about how many times I've seen these people before. If you travel enough, you'll notice that nestled there among the well-heeled flight attendants is the overworked business traveler; the couple traveling overseas for the first time; the family with a baby or a toddler…or two; the way too friendly and overly talkative flyer; the lovebirds; the prepared flyer whose backpack contains what amounts to a fully stocked grocery store shelf; and the slob—the person whose immediate area is a whirling dervish of trash and crumbs. The gang was all here. And as our plane made its way to cruising altitude, this melting pot of travelers sat blissfully unaware that life thirty-five thousand feet below was about to change in ways none of us could have seen coming. Who could know that in twelve days the entire world would be in the throes of a worldwide pandemic?

We'd just made our way across Portugal and the plane was now headed out over the ocean toward home. I was looking forward to getting home to Houston, and all that stood between me and my own bed was this flight, a short layover in Newark, and a flight to George Bush Intercontinental Airport.

But just as I reclined my seat, the overhead speakers crackled to life—"Ladies and gentlemen, from the flight deck, this is the captain speaking. We have an unforeseen medical emergency with one of our flight crew. We'll be diverting to Porto, Portugal. We apologize for the inconvenience…" I don't remember much of what the captain said after that, but I knew I wasn't getting home that night. I do recall the mur-

muring of my fellow passengers, who, like me, were shocked and more than a little upset. They all wanted to get home too.

So, on February 29, 2020, a loaded United Airlines jet headed for the United States from Madrid, Spain, landed in the coastal city of Porto, Portugal. Now, this is a city known for its incredible wine, the aptly named, "port" wine, so why not make the best of it? The airline told us we'd have a one-night layover, and that the flight crew member we'd landed for, who they thought might be having a stroke, was going to be okay. So I decided to visit a Michelin star restaurant for dinner and a bottle of port.

On that day, Spain had a reported three cases of COVID-19. By the time I stepped back onto the plane twenty-four hours later, that number had exploded to one thousand—not that any of us took note as we jetted westward.

The next couple of weeks would change that. By March 12, COVID-19 had become such an enormous problem world-wide that the World Health Organization was left with little choice but to formally declare COVID-19 a global pandemic.

Back at home in Texas, like most everyone across the country and around the world, I watched helplessly as governments—local, state, and national—without any sort of discernment, indiscriminately shut down just about everything. They ordered people to stay home, forced people to wear masks, and made church services illegal. Dictatorial leaders determined which businesses were "essential" and closed the rest. They'd launched an all-out assault on the working class. "Mom and pop" businesses were destroyed while corporate behemoths grew even bigger.

It should also be noted that for anyone who has opened a business, that business is essential to them. In fact, *all* business is essential.

Goya was allowed to operate its facilities because we're an essential business as a food producer. I was grateful for several reasons, not the least of which was that we employ more than four thousand people, most of them with families, and all of them with bills to pay.

As Goya's CEO, I now had the challenge of navigating our business through uncharted territory. The way in which the country was shut down was without precedent in the modern age. There wasn't any sort of playbook to follow. At Goya we said to our people, La Gran Familia Goya, "Our country needs us. What say you?" Our people, at every one of our facilities all around the world, said one thing, "If we don't do it, who will?" Goya employees showed incredible courage in the face of all the fear being spread.

During the first part of 2020 when COVID-19 was spreading in other parts of the world, I saw that a food shortage might be coming so at Goya we built a war chest of product—three months' worth of inventory. Once the pandemic hit, it was gone in three *weeks*.

But we had hit the ground running. We moved our machinery and our processing. We eliminated different sizes to avoid changeovers and to be more efficient. For example, we'd run one particular size of beans so we could run the machine day and night. We had to streamline the process just to keep up. We were selling roughly four times what we normally sold because nobody had anything.

The supply chain was dead so we were working around the clock to meet the food needs of people worldwide. On any given day, I literally couldn't tell if it was morning or evening. I think I was working twenty-three hours a day and grabbing quick catnaps on my office sofa or, if I was lucky, in my own bed at home. It was a lot like the early days of Goya when my father and his brothers would also work around the clock. My Uncle Frank once told me about this one time when he was running our Puerto Rico facility, when it was around two or three in the morning and he's sitting on the bed half-dressed. He's got one sock on, and he's so exhausted he asks himself, "Am I getting up or am I going to bed?"

That's what it was like for Goya during the pandemic.

At the start of the pandemic, I spent most of my time working at our Texas facility in Brookshire, which is about forty minutes west of downtown Houston. I was grateful that I didn't live too far from the plant since, as anyone familiar with Houston's near-legendary traffic issues knows, navigating Interstate 10 during the morning commute is almost always, nay, *always*, a mind-numbing exercise in futility. It was particularly odd in the early days of the pandemic, as I'd be on an overpass crossing Interstate 10 and look over to see how it was now wide-open and traffic-free. That was attributable mostly to the fact that much of society was now working remotely from home—the ones still employed, anyway. The world was closed, quite literally closed.

At the time, President Trump, who obviously is not an expert on infectious diseases, placed his trust in the head of the National Institute of Allergy and Infectious Diseases,

Dr. Anthony Fauci, who was a member of the White House Coronavirus Task Force, to provide guidance. All of us know how well that worked out.

People cast aside their constitutionally protected rights because the leftist machine scared them to death. CNN actually kept a coronavirus death count ticker displayed on its screen. I've read the Constitution of the United States and nowhere in it does it say that we're free unless there's a virus with a more than 98 percent rate of recovery. Interestingly, four years after the start of the pandemic, in March of 2024, the Centers for Disease Control and Prevention (CDC) issued new guidelines that basically said to go ahead and treat COVID-19 like the flu. The free-thinking "deplorables" had been saying that for four years! It was a containable threat, at least until the virus became politicized. Power elites had no concern for the countless lives they ruined or the businesses they destroyed.

I think Kenneth Roth, the former longtime executive director of Human Rights Watch, said it best, and this was when the pandemic was in its infancy. "For authoritarian-minded leaders, the coronavirus crisis is offering a convenient pretext to silence critics and consolidate power.... The health crisis will inevitably subside, but autocratic governments' dangerous expansion of power may be one of the pandemic's most enduring legacies."[21]

The left-wing establishment had an unquenchable thirst for power (it still does) and to achieve what it wanted, it had

---

21   Kenneth Roth, "How Authoritarians Are Exploiting the COVID-19 Crisis to Grab Power," *New York Review of Books*, April 3, 2020.

to eliminate Donald Trump from power. 2020 was an election year, so what better way to upend him than to destroy the record-setting economy he'd built? Or to create widespread unemployment when he'd achieved record-low levels of unemployment? Then liberal extremists furthered the political divide by telling people who refused a vaccine that they were menaces—getting everyone else sick—or that they were the reason for the "deadly plague." Even worse, the unvaccinated were called "murderers."

It wasn't just enough to ruin all of the accomplishments Trump had made, to destroy life as we knew it, and then hope the voters turned on the president at the ballot box. No, the liberal establishment wanted even more control over the election itself. That's why some totalitarian governors, using the pandemic as an excuse, unilaterally changed their state's election laws to allow people to vote by mail. The problem with this wasn't just that election integrity couldn't be guaranteed, but that it was unconstitutional! Only a state legislature can change its state's election laws, and not any singular elected official. Remember, I myself received two ballots in the mail. So clearly, election integrity went out the window with mail-in voting. What's particularly curious is how these officials cited health safety at the polling locations as the reasoning for mail-in voting, yet none of them seemed concerned with health safety during the violent Antifa and Black Lives Matter protests of 2020. By the way, logic dictates that if a person could stand in line at the grocery store during the pandemic, they could do the same at a polling location.

After the election was over, and it appeared some swing states may have played a little sleight of hand with the mail-in ballots, the extreme Left won. They'd eliminated Donald Trump.

When Joe Biden took over on January 20, 2021, he signed more than forty executive orders on that first day to begin his mission of unraveling everything—every success of the Trump administration. Under Trump we'd enjoyed energy independence and low gasoline prices, so naturally, Biden launched an immediate war on fossil fuels. Trump built a robust economy. Biden implemented policies to dismantle it. We had the most secure southern border in history. Biden opened it. Skyrocketing crime? Biden. Sex traffickers? Biden. Five-dollar gasoline? Biden.

As maddening as it's been, it was also to be expected. A couple of weeks before Biden took office, I was having lunch in Houston with Mark Geist, who you may remember as one of the heroes of Benghazi, and my friend Gary Heavin, the founder of Curves International and a devout man of God. We were talking about the election and its scheduled certification the next day—January 6, 2021. Yes, the famous day of the Capitol protest that the mainstream media ignorantly and falsely labeled an "insurrection." There'd been growing calls for the House to hold off on certifying the results until the widespread reports of election irregularities in some states could be investigated. As we were eating, I asked Gary what he thought, you know, whether Trump would prevail in the matter. He looked me square in the eye and said, "No, God spoke to me and He said the US isn't ready yet. We have to suffer more." What a downer thing to hear but Gary's revelation did come to pass. Trump did not prevail and the United States has most assuredly suffered as a result.

Are we ready now?!

Yes, we are.

As Trump told the gathered crowd at the AFPI Policy Summit, "America's story is far from over. We are just getting *ready* for an incredible comeback—a comeback we have no choice but to make. We won't have a country if we don't make it." As this book went to press, Trump had destroyed all of the GOP field of presidential candidates and was well on his way to securing the delegate count to win the party's nomination.

Most decent Americans have tired of suffering through the failures of the Biden administration, which are too numerous to list in the limited space of this book. A country such as ours requires strong leadership. We've had many in our history, such as Abraham Lincoln, who understood the importance of a nation being united under God. Dr. Martin Luther King Jr. was an extraordinary leader, a man of great passion and conviction, a minister of deep faith who shared his remarkable dream so that we'd become people of character who love and respect each other. Ronald Reagan knew the importance of freedom and global democracy, the power of faith, and the effectiveness of peace through strength. And of course, Donald Trump, who we were "blessed" to have as president. All of these leaders were visionaries and builders with a deep love for our America!

The country is going through an existential crisis morally, and godly leadership, guided by the Holy Spirit, is the only thing that will course correct it. One night early in the 2024 election season I'd been watching a debate of all the GOP presidential candidates (except for Trump, who didn't participate) and every one of them said the same thing, that the family is being destroyed. It's true we all must throw away the hate, look beyond the selfies, and care about the things that matter—God and family.

There's a silent majority of patriots who believe this, and it isn't so silent anymore. Extremist liberalism overplayed its hand. It thought it could endlessly push its evil ideologies and that everyone would accept them lock, stock, and barrel. Nope. Not anymore. Even the people who voted for Biden have awakened to the truth. They're rejecting him and his failed policies in large numbers—not unlike the Argentinians who rejected socialism and voted for a freedom-loving populist like Javier Milei to be their president. The now awakened people on the American Left are now getting it. They want answers to things like how we can afford to give Ukraine money but not Americans. How can we afford to give illegal immigrants debit cards, luxury hotel stays, and free college tuition?

We're taking back America.

Saint Luke, in the book of Acts, wrote, "From one man He made all the nations, that they should inhabit the whole earth; and He marked out their appointed times in history and the boundaries of their lands. God did this so that they would seek Him and perhaps reach out for Him and find Him, though he is not far from any one of us." See, God created America, as he did all nations. He wants us to reach out to Him. America must return to God.

I believe that will happen and I see one man leading America there—Donald Trump. And I believe his words from the AFPI Policy Summit. We will take back our country. "Through strength we will restore safety. Through hard work we will rebuild our prosperity. Through courage we will reclaim our liberty. Through love we will repair unity. Through success we will rediscover our pride. And through unyielding determination together, we will make America stronger, safer, greater, and more glorious than ever before."

And remember these familiar words—we are all truly *blessed* to have a leader like Donald Trump, who is a builder, and that's what my grandfather did. He came to this country to build, to grow, to prosper. And so, we have an incredible builder, and we pray, we pray for our leadership, and we pray for our country, that we will continue to prosper, and to grow.

God bless the United States of America.

CONCLUSION

"**B**lessed." Sometimes I truly cannot fathom how one word could change my life so profoundly. The Holy Spirit put that word on my lips in 2020 and, quite literally, everything that has happened to me since—every opportunity, every platform, and the seemingly impossible series of events—is a direct result of my obedience in saying that one word.

God has huge plans for our country.

As I've said many times in the past and will continue to say in the future, I believe America is the greatest country in the history of humanity. Despite what ungrateful people will tell you, it is truly the land of the free. America is the land of opportunity. Ronald Reagan once said, "America is a shining city upon a hill whose beacon light guides freedom-loving people everywhere." He was right. America is exceptional. It has a special calling and a divine purpose.

I'm hopeful most Americans embrace our exceptionalism. But we do wage an internal war with the bad seeds who've been working day and night to destroy the very things that make America exceptional.

There's a power elite, who, along with the minions of their ideology, want nothing more than to shred the fabric of our country, strip away God, and reduce America to the likes of Venezuela or Cuba. We're on the cusp of becoming a banana republic—a third world country. Who would want that? The evil and the stupid, that's who.

The few want to control the many. At the end of the day that's really what all of this is about. They love power more than they love America. They hate God, morality, decency, and integrity. And they hate Donald Trump more than they love this country if they even love it at all.

The twisted ideologies have spread through the innards of our government like a cancer. From the Oval Office to the FBI's J. Edgar Hoover Building, from the Department of Justice to the halls of Congress, from biased judges to leftist prosecutors, these people have worked in tandem to destroy America. They do it because they hate America and everything she stands for. And they hate you.

The United States is engaged in a civil war for its soul. It's good versus evil. It's freedom versus tyranny.

An America that allows an administration to arrest journalists for reporting the truth, as they did to an investigative reporter from Blaze News named Steve Baker, who'd been reporting at length on the January 6th protest at the Capitol, isn't America at all. Baker was actually handcuffed and led into court in leg chains. Former CBS News national security reporter Catherine Herridge was held in contempt of court in 2024 for refusing to reveal her sources for a series of stories she did in 2017 when she worked for Fox News. Most everyone knows, especially judges, that protecting sources is one of the tenets of journalism—a huge one. It didn't matter. The thing about Herridge is that even after she moved to CBS from Fox, she continued her unbiased reporting. Unlike most of the left-wing reporters at CBS News, she wasn't afraid to report on the many exploits of Hunter Biden, or Joe Biden's mental fitness after a special-counsel report exposed his lack of acuity.

Not uncoincidentally, CBS laid off Herridge in 2024.

When the United States government can flagrantly disregard the First Amendment and jail journalists or bury them with legal fees for reporting on the things it doesn't like, that's not an America at all.

Or consider how several blue states tried to keep Donald Trump off the 2024 ballot by claiming he was part of the so-called "insurrection" on January 6th. The power elites on the left know Biden can't beat Trump on the issues, so they tried to illegally remove Trump as a choice. They're terrified. The State of Colorado's attempt to kick Trump off the ballot went all the way to the Supreme Court of the United States, which, to the dismay of Biden and his supporters, ruled unanimously in Trump's favor. For all intents and purposes, the decision rendered moot the desire of roughly thirty states who wanted to do what Colorado tried to do. Trump responded in a post on social media calling the ruling a "BIG WIN FOR AMERICA!"

This, of course, was meant to be! This is divine intervention. The relentless attacks on Donald Trump are from the evil one trying to devour our lives, our country, and our civilization. He didn't count on Trump, and any of us, for that matter, being shielded by a cloak of protection provided by the Holy Spirit.

It is from God.

This is not unlike what happened to me and Goya. After the Holy Spirit invoked the word "blessed" in the Rose Garden, the evil one looked to cancel, attack, and boycott Goya. But the Holy Spirit threw the cloak of protection over the company and me, and He created a "buy-cott" that blessed the company. God then gave me a platform to do what He called me to do, and to say what needs to be said—that we all are called to move closer to Him.

The Holy Spirit is speaking through those who believe. The relentless attacks against Donald Trump and conservatives reveal the resounding evil of extreme progressives—the ones who hate America. But thankfully, as a result, many people have become even more resolute in their faith.

When I think of the Goya "buy-cott," I know it wasn't man-made. It was divine. We make plans, and God laughs. Nothing that has happened to me and Goya would've happened without God's intervention—without "Blessed!"

The Supreme Court ruling on the Colorado ballots didn't happen by chance. I believe God is in the 2024 election. He values each of us. He calls us by name. He's calling us all to seek salvation and to return to Him. We're engaged in a spiritual war for the heart and soul of America—a war that's intensifying.

I don't think God cares much about what political party we belong to. He cares that we have a relationship with Him. He cares that we live according to His principles. He cares that we love our neighbor as we love ourselves. He cares that we value life.

Pray for the divine protection of the Holy Spirit. If America's power elite can continue to falsely accuse Donald Trump of nefarious conduct, drag him through the courts, and try to destroy him, his business, and his family, imagine what they can do to you. You see, they're afraid of you. They're afraid of your voice and your power to influence change, be it at the ballot box or in your community. There's an old saying, "The enemy isn't fighting you because you're weak, he's fighting you because you're strong."

Be the resistance. Call upon the Holy Spirit for He will shield you.

Revival is nigh!

Late in 2023, I attended a get-together hosted by Rick Figueroa, the chair of the Texas Commission of Licensing and Regulation, at his ranch in Brenham, Texas. I'd first met him at the White House in 2020 and I would later get involved his organization, the Hispanic Impact Panel, which, as the name implies, advances conservative policies to impact Hispanic communities. At some point during the afternoon, I got to talking with Irma Aguirre, the fiancée of James Campos, the former director of the Office of Economic Impact and Diversity in the Department of Energy under Secretary Rick Perry.

Irma told me this incredible story about how after President Trump had nominated James for the position, he'd been nervously awaiting his confirmation. James very much wanted the job but was worried about whether he'd actually be confirmed. Then one seemingly quiet morning, Irma's housekeeper, Marcela, a wonderful woman of faith, told her how she'd been fervently praying since seeing the worry in James's face and had received a word from the Lord, "Don't worry, the papers are on the president's desk." A week or two later they got the call saying exactly that.

I was blown away by that story, and I asked Irma if Marcela had any opinion on President Trump running for office again. Irma related that Marcela confidently and without any doubt or hesitation, told her how while in prayer, God told her Donald Trump would win the election in 2024.

Sometimes God uses the humblest of people to trumpet the most profound of messages. And Marcela isn't the only one. Remember, Tom Zimmer, the mythic Hermit of Loretto prophesied, "The man who, in the future, is going to lead America back to God, is Donald J. Trump." Pastor Mario Bramnick of New Wine Ministries in Florida, has said, "God has his hands on Donald J. Trump, and he isn't letting go."

Heed my words—

In 2024 Donald J. Trump will once again be elected president of the United States.

I've written about the phrase in the book of Esther that says, "...for such a time as this."

This. Is. The. Time.

We are on the precipice of spiritual greatness—of making a profound difference for our country, not just for this generation, but also for those to come. The Holy Spirit has called us—you, me, and, yes, Donald Trump, to a mission of bringing our country closer to God and winning this spiritual war. As we embark on this mission, hold dear the words of the Apostle Paul, "We are hard pressed on every side, but not crushed; perplexed, but not in despair; persecuted, but not abandoned; struck down, but not destroyed."

No matter how difficult the attack, be like Trump and never give up.

And never forget—we are blessed.

ACKNOWLEDGMENTS

One must begin and acknowledge that we are called by name, loved, valued, and blessed by God our Creator. God gave the gift of life to me and my five brothers and sisters through our amazing parents, Anthony and Betty. He further blessed me with six incredible children, their spouses, and fourteen grandchildren. I could not achieve anything without their incomparable support, encouragement, and love. After God, my family is the single most important thing in my life. I am grateful for each and every one of them.

My Uncle Frank—I could never thank him enough for the unselfish ways he helped me through the most trying times in my life. After Dad and Mom passed, Frank took me under his wing and loved, nurtured, and guided me as his own son. He's been gone for twenty-two years now, but I will never forget everything he did for me and the part he played in helping to shape me into the man I am today.

True friends are forever, and I am blessed by Suvajit Basu, his beautiful wife, and talented son. I'm also so grateful for my other lifelong friend, Vinny Arsi, his five cowboys, and their families.

I never intended to write this book, however, I was compelled by the Holy Spirit and encouraged by Ally

Brito and Dave Erickson to tell my story. They've been invaluable in helping me to do just that.

I give thanks to God and His Holy Spirit who placed the word "blessed" on my lips that day at the White House. We were, and are, truly blessed by President Donald Trump and his family. He will lead this country closer to God because he is cloaked with the courage of the Holy Spirit.

I never would have ended up at the White House on July 9, 2020; never been named as part of the White House Commission for Hispanic Prosperity; never been in a position to offer millions of pounds of food to President Trump for a nation in crisis during the COVID-19 pandemic, were it not for a few very special people. Syddia Lee-Chee has worked with me for years and I am grateful for all she's done. She is the one who coordinated our gift of food for the American people through her contacts in the White House. She also saw the need also for a Hispanic connection between the Trump administration and the Latino community.

Syddia worked with the talented deputy director and special assistant to the president at the White House, Jenny Korn, along with policy advisor/special assistant to the president/director of Hispanic outreach, Dr. Andrea (Reyes) Ramirez, to bridge the gap and foster our special relationship with the Trump administration. Through it all, I cannot say enough about the incredible professionalism of President Trump's administrative assistant, Molly Michael.

I was honored to have served with many great Americans who were part of the commission such as the Honorable Daniel Cortez, the Honorable Mario Rodriguez (Hispanic 100), the

Honorable Casandra (Cassy) Garcia, the Honorable Jovita Carranza of the US Small Business Administration, and others such as my good friend, Eduardo Verástegui.

I want to especially acknowledge someone who was there at the Rose Garden in 2020 when I made my "blessed" comments—renowned neurosurgeon, 2016 presidential candidate, mentor, and friend, Dr. Benjamin Carson, the former secretary of the Department of Housing and Urban Development. He has been a tremendous supporter, confidant, and just a fantastic man of God who has blessed me more times than I can count.

Dr. Carson would later ask me to become a founding member of his newly formed America Cornerstone Institute (ACI) with the "cornerstones" of community, faith, liberty, and life! I'm honored and grateful to work with their incredible executive team: ACI cofounder, the lovely and talented Candy Carson, CEO Andrew Hughes, COO Drew McCall, CDO Michael Burley, Irvin Dennis, Belsis Romero, Little Patriot Trip Burley, and many others who seek to fortify the cornerstones that have built America and made her strong.

The exposure I received after the Rose Garden event caught the eyes of Brooke Rollins and Linda McMahon who were forming The America First Policy Institute (AFPI) which champions the values and ideals of America. They asked me to join as a founding member. I am now part of an illustrious group of patriots that, in three short years, has put AFPI at the forefront of US conservative policy. These people have become family to me: Newt Gingrich, Larry Kudlow, Chad Wolf, Alveda King, General Keith Kellogg, Jack Brewer,

Martin Gillespie, Ashley Hayek, Tim Dunn, past Cabinet members, and an incredible staff that is so incredibly talented and successful!

The incomparable teachings of Saint Mother Teresa of Calcutta, and the film that I was privileged to be a part of, *Sound of Freedom*, were the impetus and inspiration for Goya Cares. I am so grateful to be playing at least a small part in helping to improve the lives of so many innocent people hurt by the horrors of trafficking, and I thank all of the organizations in the Goya Cares coalition who work so hard helping the people who so desperately need it.

I want to give thanks to the entire team of people who've made both Goya Cares and *Sound of Freedom* so successful—Rafael and Meiling Toro, Mayte Sera Weitzman and Javier Weitzman, Luz Damaris Rosario and Julian Rodriguez, Maricela Baez, Justa Silva, Elsa and Charles Ezell, Amelia Hebert, Ally Brito, Syddia Lee-Chee, Natalie Maniscalco, Jennifer Holman, Eyes On Me (Dennis Turnipseed, Bobby Herring, Ryan Orbin), Gabby Baptista, Aaron Morgado, Adrianna Calhoon, Eduardo Verástegui, Jim Caviezel, Tim and Katherine Ballard, José Antonio Fernandez, Bob Cunningham, Kathy Gibbons, Becca Carey, Macee Barber, Sara Carter, Lara Logan, María Angelica Cuellar, Zach and Leslie Helmut, John and Margo Catsimatidis, Rita Cosby, Carlos Vives, Henry Cardenas, Marc Anthony, Patrick Kelly (Supreme Knight USA).

My team and I made, not one, but two trips to Poland to bring hope to the refugees of Ukraine and to help the wonderful, selfless people doing God's work to help the victims of trafficking. All of them are special people and deserve our gratitude—Michael Capponi of Global Empowerment Mission, Jeremy Loch (ARIEL), Adriana Calhoon, and Nelia and Andrii Shkut. We also received guidance, love, and protection from Father Jon Kalisch OP and Szymon Czyszek of the Knights of Columbus.

I can't say enough good things about Sister Teresa de la Fuente of the Sisters of Our Lady of Mercy at the Divine Mercy Shrine in Kraków. She and the congregation care for trafficked children and women and they graciously received our Goya Cares contingent which was carrying thousands of rosaries for the people of Ukraine and Poland.

"The Miracle of the Rosaries" would never have happened without the spark provided by the amazing Shannon Haase of San Antonio, Texas. What an incredible woman of faith and a truly humble servant of God. I want to give thanks to Archbishop Gustavo García-Siller of the Archdiocese of San Antonio, Texas, Father Dat Hoang of Saint Faustina Catholic Church in Fulshear, Texas, and Archbishop Wacław Tomasz Depo in Częstochowa, Poland, each of whom blessed the thousands of rosaries we took to Ukraine and Poland.

Last, but certainly not the least in any way, I am so grateful for La Gran Familia Goya. Thank you for everything that you do each and every day. And to the one who started it all, Don Prudencio Unanue—Gracias Abuelo por todo. Te amo y te extraño.

ABOUT THE AUTHOR

Bob Unanue is the president and chief executive officer of Goya Foods, the largest Hispanic-owned food company in the United States. His career at Goya spans over forty-five years, where he began at a young age learning all facets of the business—from production and delivery to warehousing and administration. Under his leadership, Goya has grown significantly, reaching new markets and distribution channels, and helping to increase brand awareness and product demand among new consumers.

Unanue created the Goya Gives initiative, supporting hundreds of nonprofit organizations, events, scholarships, and giving programs around the world, and he launched Goya Cares, a global initiative dedicated to combating child trafficking and raising awareness of mental health issues among teens. Unanue was also executive producer of the hit movie, *Sound of Freedom*, that helped to raise awareness about trafficking.

Unanue has received various business and humanitarian awards for his dedication to the community. In 2020, he was appointed to the White House Commission for Hispanic Prosperity. He is a founding board member of the America First Policy Institute and chairman of the Hispanic Leadership Coalition. Unanue serves as a cornerstone trustee for the American Cornerstone Institute and sits on the boards of the Maestro Cares Foundation and Culinary Institute of America.

After using the word "blessed" at the White House on July 9, 2020, Unanue has become a sought-after conservative voice and frequently appears on national media outlets to discuss high-profile national and international issues.

He graduated from Merrimack College with a degree in accounting and studied at the University of Seville in Spain. Unanue currently resides in Houston, Texas, and takes great pride in spending quality time with his six children and fourteen grandchildren, and his two wildly energetic and lovable pups, Arfi and Braco.

"WHAT YOU SPEND YEARS BUILDING MAY BE
DESTROYED OVERNIGHT, BUILD IT ANYWAY."

—MOTHER TERESA

Bob Unanue